THE INVISIBLE PRISON

The Invisible Prison
First published in 2009 by
The Dedalus Press
13 Moyclare Road
Baldoyle
Dublin 13
Ireland

www.dedaluspress.com

ISBN 978 1 906614 15 7 (paperback)
ISBN 978 1 906614 16 4 (hardbound)

Dedalus Press titles are represented in North America
by Syracuse University Press, Inc., 621 Skytop Road,
Suite 110, Syracuse, New York 13244, and in the UK by
Central Books, 99 Wallis Road, London E9 5LN

The Dedalus Press receives financial assistance from
The Arts Council / An Chomhairle Ealaíon

Printed in Ireland by Colour Books Ltd.

THE INVISIBLE PRISON
Scenes from an Irish Childhood

Pat Boran

DEDALUS PRESS
DUBLIN, IRELAND

ACKNOWLEDGEMENTS

Acknowledgements are due to the editors/producers of the following in which many of these pieces, or versions, originally appeared:

The History of Irish Tennis (ed. Tom Higgins); *The Letterbox* (Arts Office, Laois County Council); *The Irish Times Magazine, New Hibernia Review* (USA) and *The Quiet Quarter*, Lyric FM. A number of these pieces have also been collected in anthologies of contributions to the RTÉ Radio 1 programme, *Sunday Miscellany*, edited by Cliodhna Ní Anluain. Special thanks are due to a number of producers of *Sunday Miscellany* over the years, among them Lorelei Harris (now Editor of Features, Arts and Drama), Martha McCarron, Liz Sweeney and in particular Cliodhna Ní Anluain who not only gave a good number of these pieces their first 'outing' but also connected me to the audience whose responses prompted the idea for this book.

Grateful thanks are due to Muireann Ní Chonaill, Arts Officer, and her employers at Laois County Council, in particular for the inaugural Laois Artists Patronage Award in 2006, which enabled work on this book; also to Gerry Maher, County Librarian, and Marguerite Gibson and all the staff of Portlaoise Library for their welcome and assistance.

To Brendan and Brian McNamara and the many members of Portlaoise Choral Society for inviting me to read some of these pieces in Portlaoise in December 2007 at an event which is likely to remain one of my fondest memories of the town..

To John and Denise (Curtin) Dunne for their friendship and encouragement in my various literary endeavours over the years.

And finally to Mary Ledwidge who, in 1981/2, as part of a VEC Secretarial Course, managed to teach me to type—that is, me, my friend Michael Larkin and, oh yes, about 40 teenage girls! Seldom before or since has the Muse faced such stiff competition!

To my family and friends
who, so far, have put up with it

Contents

"There must be some way out of here," said the joker to the thief.
—Bob Dylan, 'All Along the Watchtower', 1968

Where the Prison Is

It is cold. So cold I can see my breath. The engine of my father's Volkswagen van turns over, but the heater it is meant to drive has long since given up the ghost. I pull my duffle coat tight around me, rub my hands together, count to a hundred, then from a hundred back to one, then to a hundred again.

In the winter dark, beyond the windscreen, beyond the glistening frost-capped lawn revealed in the headlights, there is a country house, or a house in the countryside, or a house at the edge of a town, and through the wooden doorframe we have just delivered I can just about make out my father, still talking, still shaking hands, all the while slowly backing out.

On our way back home the roads are treacherous and my father proceeds at a cautious pace, the loadless van much lighter now and no doubt far less stable on the icy roads.

A couple of miles from town he slows down even further. There is a figure standing by the side of the road on a grass verge less than a foot wide, one of those new luminous armbands the only thing in that moment keeping him alive.

My father tells me to roll down my window. The stranger approaches. He looks shocked to find himself caught out in the dark. My father eyes him closely, decides in a moment, gives me a nod.

I open the door.

The stranger sits in.

"Where you headed?" he says in a hard-to-place accent, part local, part, well, somewhere else.

My father looks him over again in the relative light.

"Portlaoise," he says. "Any good to you?"

"Ah," says the stranger with a smile, "where the prison is."

The Rock of? Cashel.

The Cliffs of? Moher.

The Great Wall of? China.

Equally significant, equally undeniable, from the early 1970s Portlaoise is where the prison is. If you switch on the radio or television on almost any day and hear the name of the town mentioned you can be sure you've tuned into yet another story of prisoner transfers, mass protests or, now and again, attempted or even successful escapes. As far as the world is concerned, the town and the prison, the prison and the town, are one and the same.

Tourists passing through enquire about our most famous building, wanting to photograph it (despite the warnings). And more than once the BBC television news (seen in someone else's house) has shown a map of the country with nothing but the prison at its heart.

"Have you ever seen that map," the stranger says, "by Ptolemy the Greek cartographer, 2nd century AD, I think, almost nothing on it to the west of Dublin but Dunum—" He sees we're not following. "You know, the Rock of Dunamase?"

My father nods to himself but says nothing. Maybe it's one of those adult questions where you only have to hum and nod. I hum and nod, too. After all, the only famous map I know is the 3D papier mâché one my classmate Louis Byrne and I made one day in primary school and which my father put in our Main Street travel agency window for the whole town to see. No prison on that or ruined castle of Dunamase. Whatever that might mean.

People often end up in Portlaoise through no choice of their own—the prisoners, of course, but their relatives too, coming from all over the country, and all over the island… Then there are the drivers travelling between Dublin and Limerick or Dublin and Cork: caught in the traffic jam that is the town, rather than lose the will to live they pull up outside Egan's in the lower square or Grey's in the upper, hoping that the congestion will have eased during the course of a leisurely meal and some gentle probing about where they're headed, where they come from, and if they might know such-and-such or so-and-so from there.

However, few disappointments compare to that on the faces of those who arrive by CIE coach, and in great numbers, every August Bank Holiday Monday without fail, on the occasion of the CIE Mystery Tour, the kids laden down with buckets and spades pacing up and down the deserted Main Street, trying to puzzle out where the sea might be down half a dozen narrow side lanes.

Portlaoise is where the prison is, and little else. Even us local youngsters who dream, as all youngsters do, of heading off, of getting away, even we keep a mental bag packed underneath our beds, as if waiting for the secret signal that the guards are asleep, the keys dangling visibly from their pocket-chains.

"Where the prison is," says the proprietor of a Dublin record shop in 1980 when I'm up for the day buying punk records, a *London Calling* or Killing Joke T-shirt.

"Where the prison is?" says a French teenager in Lourdes in 1977, striking up a conversation when he sees me moping around the town.

"Do you know much about it, the prison?" asks this stranger now, sitting with my father and myself in the cab of the van, following our two probing headlight beams in off the bog and back towards our midland town.

For a moment all three of us are quiet. My father adjusts the rear-view mirror and then I notice it's me he's looking now. He seems to have realised that something odd is going on here. It's written in his eyes. For the fact is, it's still just 1970, and in 1970 talk of the prison is not something you hear every day: there are still other prisons in the land, and there is still a Portlaoise which is not synonymous with its prison. For some of our friends who live right up close to it, the prison is just a wall at the end of the garden against which to play handball until dark.

"You're not writing a book, are you?" my father says, seeing me reach to take out a school copybook and pen.

Actually I am just thinking of trying to finish my homework. But before I can figure out how to respond to him, it's the stranger who answers.

"I'll admit it's occurred to me," he says.

He touches the St Christopher medal on the dashboard, watches my father's hand change down then back up a gear, smiles again, first at my father, then at me.

"About?" My father is looking straight ahead of him again, following the curve of the road.

"The usual stuff, I suppose." The stranger shrugs. "The town, childhood, school, the prison…" When my father says nothing, he goes on: "Music, girls, my mother, you…" I'm sure that's what he says, though it's hard to hear above the noise.

My father sits there, nodding to himself. Then the rumble of the engine starts to seduce him and soon he's happily humming along, maybe thinking of the deal he's just managed to close.

"Oh give me land, lots of land, under starry skies above," he croons, "don't fence me in…"

First Non-Memory

I am looking at the sky, lying in my pram in our back garden. Around me voices, laughter, the buzzing of busy little bees. Now and then a face peers in and down, my older sisters or brother, calling me Lick Show already, letting me hold and squeeze their thumbs in my puny fists.

But there are long periods where it's just me and the sky above me, blue and clear, and I can feel heat on my face, the tickle of a lacy cover against my skin, on the inside of the pram the cool of a nipple-like stud that holds the folding hood in place...

It is—it has to be—the summer of 1964, which makes me not quite nine months old.

The other possibility is that I remember nothing at all, that all of this is imagined, and imagined for so long that what I remember now is a jigsaw, a montage, a mosaic of fragments drawn from family photo albums, the reports of siblings and the glitter-spray of memory.

How does one distinguish between what one remembers and what one remembers imagining?

And could it be true, as some people claim, that a baby in a pram can remember nothing at all.

I can't believe it. I won't believe it. After all, I remember my mother's breast, her voice, her heartbeat, her womb, her blood, her breathing, I remember her egg, my father's sperm swimming to meet it...

For I was present, was I not, though neither egg nor sperm, neither here nor there, floating in the ether as I'll float again when it all winds down, when the last page is written and the last words are read and I am stretched again in an open bed, the sky above me, the garden trembling, disembodied voices singing the song of home.

Hardware and Software

In the mid 1950s, when computers were still the stuff of science fiction and the word 'software'—had it been known—could only have meant the kind of women's underclothing to be found in the deepest recesses of Burke's Drapery on Main Street, the known world (Portlaoise included) was indisputably the domain of hardware.

In every town and in most of the larger villages, alongside churches and pubs, hardware shops were a guaranteed presence, the crucial, civilizing ingredient, and often occupied pride of place, their invariably enormous plate-glass windows, large as cinema screens, offering 24-hour views to a treasure trove of daunting tools and dark alchemical wonders. From the particle physics of nuts and screw and washers, through the weapon-like spades and forks, rat-traps and poisons, to (in central place and always in a well-planned, well-maintained exhibit) the ferocious jaws and teeth of a range of cutting implements whose affront to the flesh was, even in passing, beyond doubt—hardware ruled the world.

In my mother's case, indeed, hardware was the world. Born in Tullamore, Co. Offaly, while not yet in her teens she had left her family in Roscrea, Co. Tipperary to be raised by her uncle and aunt in Maryborough (or Port Leix), moving in with them into their Main Street home and hardware business. After completing her Intermediate Certificate in the Presentation Convent, she took a secretarial course and worked in the courthouse just across the street for about a year (dreaming of a job in the library) followed by 14 years in Odlums' Mills, at that time among the biggest employers in the town.

Then, in 1955, just three months apart, she found first her beloved Aunt Kitt and then her Uncle John dead in their beds, Uncle John just minutes after a bird had found its way into the house through the bathroom window, an omen whose significance my mother at once recognised...

My mother was now 32, still young but suddenly alone in a rambling 11-room house, surrounded by shadows. What would she do with such a place? What could she have done? She called up a well-known local dealer, Whelan of Stradbally, and told him to come or to send someone to come to value the rooms-full of furniture and hardware, to make her an offer that might free her from the weight of it all.

And the man who was sent to carry out the task was the man who would become her husband, and my father.

The fact that Nicholas Boran, then 38 years of age, had already spent the first half of his life working in a sequence of hardware shops—from Castlecomer, Co. Kilkenny, to Virginia, Co. Cavan, and now nearby Stradbally, Co. Laois—is an indication that he too, like so many men of his generation, had been seduced by the undeniable attractions of the tangible. My father was one of 14 children, and, where more than half of his siblings had taken holy orders, he had glimpsed sufficient potential in the near-at-hand. In fact, so in awe was my father of the ready and steady, the dependable, the potent, the not-to-be-swayed or bandied-with resistance of tools, his first meeting with my heart-broken mother must have seemed doubly unreal, doubly gifted, an unlikely miracle to receive from a god who, in those days, divided families and, not surprisingly, kept his back turned on his congregation.

Thinking of it now, the huge old house and adjoining shop and sheds—all of them full to bursting with ancient implements— my father must have felt himself to be entering a dream world, a castle magazine, armoury and apothecary's store combined. For here in every wooden drawer, tin drum and carefully weighed-out bag were the very nuts and bolts, the grains and pellets, the screws and nails and glues that held the world together and made it work. Here was the treasure trove, the epicentre of hardware, a world whose only enemies were damp and rust.

And here too, as he must almost immediately have seen, was his wife-to-be, my mother, fragile after two deaths in that house, quiet-spoken but clear, striving towards a future she wanted and deserved, determined to set out again, to start over, at the heart of that hardware paradise its dedicated software—without which it was all just lifeless junk.

The Boy from Outer Space

Though the 1960s is not all that long ago, infant mortality was still much more common that it is today. And like a lot of people of my generation, I too had an older sibling who did not survive beyond infancy.

The first Patrick or Paddy Boran (I too was almost always known as Paddy as a child) was born on 22nd August 1960 and died the following day. My mother had carried him for nine months, and then came home from the County Hospital empty-handed, broken-hearted, stunned, but with little time to dwell on her loss. Already at home she had two lively children under the age of three, and over the next four years of so three more, including my self, would follow.

I first learned of the existence of the first Paddy Boran when I was about five. His name was listed among family members in the beautiful illustrated Bible which my uncle Peter (ordained a Capuchin in the year of my birth) had given to my parents and in the final few pages of which my mother had carefully added, just after the dates of birth of all her six of her children, the date of Paddy's death. "Death should not be a tragedy for a Christian," declared the motto on the gilt-edged page, "a Christian lives for another world".

Paddy Boran. In my mother's familiar handwriting, the words seemed more than ever to form my name. I thought about him often. Though he'd lived for only that one August day ('Russia Getting Ready for Man's Flight into Outer Space' ran the headline in *The Irish Times* the morning he died), I always imagined him to be whatever age I was, travelling along through time and space on parallel lines. We grew up together, me in this world, he in his.

In a way, that sense of being shadowed, echoed, partnered, has stayed with me ever since. Though I'd already begun to do so while living in Ireland—following the prompt of a number of teachers—when I lived for a period in London in the early 1980s I usually introduced myself as Pat, put my name down as Pat when I applied for part-time work. Maybe it was a kind of emigrant's reinvention. Maybe I was trying to find a distance from myself.

As it happened, the name stuck. Not being Paddy I couldn't be a Paddy, and being Pat I found myself called for every interview I applied for, as if (as the old joke has it) by unintentionally blurring my gender I'd managed to double my chances of a date.

By the time I came back to Ireland a year later, the name fitted like a second skin.

Which might be just as well. For when my father died in 1999 my mother would have a new headstone erected over the formerly unmarked family plot. And on it, as well as the name of her beloved husband, she would include that of Patrick, her innocent infant son, watching over us ever since from his orbit in space.

Mousey

Mousey was Con Brennan's dog. Con Brennan was my father's employer, in a past more distant than we could imagine. Back there, for some extended but vaguely defined period, my father and Con Brennan's dog had come into contact with each other. Or near contact. For Mousey, having managed to contract canine distemper, in the style of the time was tied to a tree for months on end and almost went out of his mind with desire to be free and about his mousing ways.

We, little nippers that we were, had no dog of our own just yet (only our neighbours' half-blind mutt who, now we were learning to love him, limped when we wished he might run and barked when he should have been quiet). Unsurprisingly then we couldn't get enough of the tales of Mousey: he was our *Little Dorrit,* our *Man in the Iron Mask* and our *Hunchback of Notre Dame* all rolled into one. (That Mousey was also a prisoner may have helped him to tug at our heartstrings, given that even we small kids had by then noticed and begun to ask questions about the big grey building that squatted on the Dublin Road.)

What my father's tales of Mousey lacked by way of plot they made up for in graphic, even gruesome, detail—such as the unerasable image of the rope tightening about the neck of the little dog as he strained to reach his bowl or to chase a brazen cat away.

Given our ages at the time, me about 5, my brother Michael 4, my sister Mary a little short of 7, it's perhaps not surprising that I don't remember much of the individual episodes, and neither can I say if my father was a particularly good storyteller with his kids.

The truth is that for the most part we were feigning interest in poor Mousey, after the first few episodes at least, having seen the way my father, once he had embarked on a tale, could not be distracted from it.

Usually it was Mary who suggested it, almost always when it was time for bed and we wanted to stay up, even if there was nothing particular worth staying up for. "Da," she'd say, maybe winking to my brother or myself. "Tell us about Mousey again?"

Almost forty years after the events he was recalling, the mere mention of that small dog's name could take my father away from whatever he was reading in the newspaper (magnifying glass in hand like Sherlock Holmes), and pulling one or two or three of us into "the cowhouse" (as he called the space between his knees) he'd clamp us in there tight, half protection, half incarceration, and regale and hypnotize, distract and delight us with the Comer Chronicles of Mousey Brennan—until my mother called it a day and marched us up to bed, our slave chorus of "Ah, ma, just one more story…" failing to save us.

Upstairs, the bedroom growing in size as my brother drifted away from me in sleep; the house going quiet as my sister found her own path out and our older siblings made their way to their own rooms up a second floor staircase that lead to nothing else. From the kitchen below, now and then I'd hear the clang of a pot or a lid, the rush or gurgling of water, the smack-smack of a hatchet chopping turf or breaking briquettes for the range: my mother finishing her long day's work.

But many nights sleep didn't come right away and, perhaps because I was a boy, often times I lay there wondering what it was my father could be reading every night, and so late into the night, long after my mother banked up the fuel, tightened the spinner, said goodnight to my father, and the stairs had creaked and settled after her own ascent to sleep.

Once I crept down and watched him for an age from the shadows, doing nothing but reading page after page after page.

After that I could travel down simply by closing my eyes. I could float down the stairs, push open the kitchen door without a sound, without a sound cross the navy and blue-grey tiles to where he sat with the magnifying glass held stubbornly at arm's length, the newsprint letters swelling and shrinking in his lens like the language of dreams.

Scarcely breathing at all now, I would draw up close to him and from over his shoulder (no doubt as he'd done with his own father) examine the same strange words set out there, the same grim news of the world holding both of us rapt (for all the world like Con Brennan's dog) and no less tied—as I think of us now—to some great family tree.

The 'Self-Made' Man

1. Billy Butlin

Billy Butlin was a 'self-made' man. That was my father's pronouncement whenever the entrepreneur's name came up in conversation—which it was sure to do at least once a year when the gradually lengthening spring eveings turned our thoughts to summers by the sea.

In the days before package holidays on the Costa del Sol, Irish family holidays came in two main varieties, both of them taking place on Irish soil.

The first of these was the small-group affair in which a family would separate itself from the world to huddle together in a run-down cottage or decrepit caravan on a windswept stretch of coast, and in which personal differences were mercilessly amplified to the point of violence.

The second took place at Butlin's Mosney.

Bearing an unfortunate resemblance to the Nazi concentration camps 'discovered' in middle and eastern Europe just three years earlier at the end of the war, Butlin's had opened outside Drogheda in 1948 and almost immediately took the Irish holiday market by storm.

Dan Lowry's bar; the raised-up, glass-walled swimming pool where voyeurs (which was everyone) could gaze at semi-naked swimmers going past; countless dodgem cars and swinging planes; crazy golf, a boating pond and a bowling green; short-skirted waitresses and fringe-topped Redcoats; and a dune-lined beach where there was always the chance of finding unexploded rounds from the nearby military firing range at Gormanston.

And of course, at the heart of it all, laid out in almost comically tidy rows, the hundreds of two-toned, striped-curtained chalets that became home and prison, games room and love-nest to a generation of Irish holidaymakers, southern and northern, many of whom had never been anywhere else. Kids ran themselves ragged, and adults, as often as not, drank what they thought they could hold, and some more, before heading home well after midnight, knocking on maybe half a dozen identical doors—"Shut up!" "Get out of that!" "There's children asleep in here!"—before finding their own.

Billy Butlin's might not have been the world we'd been promised, but it was a world without compare.

It was also a world without precedent, certainly when it came to scale. In calling its owner a 'self-made' man, my father's phrase was intended to praise the way Butlin had built up his huge commercial empire from next-to-nothing. As a youngster, as one version of the story has it, Butlin had begun trading out of a wheelbarrow on the streets of Bristol, making his first real money running hoopla stalls in London before graduating to a string of fairgrounds and then to an eventual eight full-blown holiday camps, of which Mosney was the sole Irish concern.

For my part, though I eventually puzzled out the general meaning of my father's pronouncement, for years there would linger in my mind an image of a man, solid as might be expected from the waist up, but bent over to try to complete the fiddly bits of himself from the waist down.

Half-done and half-undone, my father's phrase placed Billy Butlin for me in the same category as the Frankenstein monster, though the latter had a mad Doctor, fiendishly complicated equipment and the timely intervention of a lightning bolt to rely on: Billy Butlin had managed it all himself.

Perhaps my fascination with the phrase had to do with the fact that, on a childhood visit to Stradbally Steam Rally the previous summer, I had seen a man on a stretcher being lifted through the open doors of an ambulance. Half-covered with a blanket (and himself looking, as the phrase has it, pale as a sheet), he too seemed to me a 'self-made' man—though to judge by the horrified expressions of the many people watching—somewhat less well finished than he might have been.

The image of a man bent over, as if trying to complete or to fix something in himself, has another connection for me to Butlin's Mosney, a connection which, in the interests of completion, I will now describe.

2. The Whistle

The whistle was a small green-and-red thing from a lucky bag. I can still see it clearly to this day though it was ever in my possession only a few minutes, and those now more than forty years ago. My younger brother, I believe, had a similar one but had already lost it or tired of it or perhaps put it away somewhere safe in other to retrieve it later, though the events of the next few minutes would almost certainly have made him rethink his plans.

What happened is that I was, as one might imagine, blowing the whistle. In fact, I think it very likely that I was blowing and blowing and blowing the whistle, with the energy a five-and-a-half-year-old boy will give to such things, surrendering to a new pleasure, to new experiment, fully, without restraint, delighting in the shrill, clear note that emanated from it.

And with this delight no doubt I blew once or twice more, very likely dancing and glancing around to see who might be watching, who might be listening, delighting as was I in my one-note staccato symphony.

It was at this point, or thereabouts, that I must have taken the decision to try to expand my repertoire. Perhaps I was temporarily distracted by the sudden appearance of a sibling or neighbour in my vicinity. Perhaps a butterfly had briefly fluttered by overhead (there still being butterflies by the dozen in our yard back then), its passing causing me to look up from my labours, to crane my neck a moment skywards and open up the doorway of my throat...

But for one reason or another, on an instrument that was, after all, designed for only one direction of airflow, as perhaps seems now inevitable I broke with convention and decided to try a single suck.

Ordinarily such a change of approach to the playing of an instrument might be expected to produce at most a modulation of the original note, at best no new note at all. In the case of a whistle with a pea inside (a cork ball pea, as was likely the case), one might expect the sucked-back pea to be dashed against the rear wall of the chamber, like a lunatic in a cage, thereafter to fall still, and silent, with the falling breath. One might, in addition, expect the force of retreating air to hold it there, frozen, for a moment, precisely in the air-stream just then exiting through the slot. One might even, conceivably, imagine a slightly wet cork ball pea (as a determinedly whistle-blowing child is liable to produce) becoming stuck in said slot and requiring a sudden flick or shake or tap or even solid thump against a larger solid object to dislodge it.

But as the gods appear to have decided, nothing so routine on this occasion, and in the end it wasn't just the pea but the whistle itself that presented the problem.

If bad luck meant I didn't simply cough at the opportune moment and expel whatever it was that had entered my mouth back the way it had come—like a small missile launched from inside a cave—good luck meant that having bounced, pinball-like, against my tonsils (this, admittedly, I may have imagined), the small interloper mercifully overshot my windpipe and like the submarine in *Fantastic Voyage* instead began its slow descent into my stomach and a touchdown in the least hospitable of all possible worlds.

Many parents say the time they worry most about their children is when nothing seems amiss. There is no shouting or screaming, none of the whooping of demented scalp-hunters in the next room or from the top of the stairs. Instead an eerie silence enters the world, a silence that is made all the more eerie for the fact that it contains children in its ambit.

Such a silence I provided that day for my hard-working mother, inside in the kitchen peeling potatoes, boiling a ham, getting the show on the road.

Suddenly it must have seemed as if the birdsong of our long back yard and the adjoining neighbours' fields had gone quiet (the sedge had withered from the lake, as Keats had it), as if the supernatural had come to call. For when she looked up, before her there stood in th doorway her middle son, his face pale, his green eyes wide, as if he had seen beyond the limits of the visible world.

It was the day before we were due to leave for our week away in Butlin's, and here was little Paddy come to tell his mother of his misfortune, his child's voice (as I imagine it now) accompanied by the faint but undeniable sound of whistling.

3. The Doctor

"You've swallowed a whistle?"

My mother's hands frame my face. She opens my mouth and looks in at the nothingness I carry inside of me.

"Are you sure?"

"I sink somesing hiss against the—" I point at it.

"Your uvula," my mother says. "I'll call Doctor Maguire..."

While I sit myself down, slowly, my mother goes to the front room and dials the number. The doctor is a family friend and a family man himself whose own lively son, almost exactly my age, has no doubt provided his own challenges to his father's medical expertise over the years. As it happens, the whistle is not only small but, fortunately, rounded at the edges. And with no sign of obstruction in my windpipe, there is after all (Doctor Maguire

21

will have put this delicately) only one direction it might now be expected to take.

To my surprise that turns out to be up the N7, through Monasterevin, Kildare, Newbridge and Naas (none of them yet bypassed) then up through Dublin, past the airport and on to Balbriggan and Gormanston, our adventure still calling us, the bright lights, the giant dining halls, that famous glass-walled pool.

4. Journey into the Unknown

> *We're off to Dublin in the green, in the green*
> *Where the helmets glisten in the sun*
> *Where the bayonets flash and the rifles crash*
> *To the rattle of a Thompson gun.*

Though among the most moderate rebels one might expect to meet, my father cannot drive us to Dublin in those last years of the 1960s—those last almost innocent years before the Troubles began—without that rebel song coming to his mind. When he drives south towards his own people's land the snatches of song that come to him are always tinged with nostalgia and regret. But Dublin-bound he becomes, one might have said had they not known him, a military man.

And so we join in, all of us singing *"And we're off to Dublin in the green, in the green"* with delight and gusto, me with one hand clasping my stomach, wondering what might be ahead of me now, as we go north and the rebel whistle makes it way inexorably south.

5. The Trouble with Holidays

Different family holidays lodge in the memory for different reasons: Ballybunion in 1973 will be the year I nearly lose my finger, belly-sliding down a grass slope and reaching for a hold into what will prove to be a pile of broken glass; Lahinch in 1979 will be the year my father, going down in the still-bright early evening to get something from the car, disturbs a would-be thief and comes close to losing an eye in the ensuing struggle.

And 1968 will always be the year of Butlin's, the week-long holiday captured in a single surviving photograph in which my father has apparently driven back to Portlaoise to work in the peace and quiet of an empty house for a few days, and the camp photographer has managed to scalp my mother.

What is most unnerving about these real and apparent accidents is that they happened when we were all on holiday, leaving our old lives behind, enjoying the illusion that we might make ourselves anew.

Did we ever go to Butlin's again? I would have to ask my mother that, as any other trips could only pale in comparison. But from among the 3,000 campers present that week, out of all those sights and sounds and tastes and smells, the only scenes I can summon up now are of my brother and myself, short sticks in hand, probing the soft dune sand in search of bullets; and, from late that first night, not so much the picture of a man bent over, as if trying to complete or repair himself, but back in the chalet, the rest of the young family asleep in their bunks, a boy and his mother, the boy looking on, powerless, in silence, his long-suffering mother down on her knees in the half-dark, searching for the shell that will tell her that her son will survive.

Dinkies

It was the day of my 5th birthday, and someone (my mother?) had given me a pair of Matchbox Dinkies, those die-cast scale-model cars that constitute first-car ownership for small boys everywhere and set the terms and reference for so many dreams and ambitions.

What exactly it was about those particular cars (a Green E-Type Jaguar, a white Triumph Stag) that so engrossed me, it's difficult now to say, but for hours and hours, from the very moment I took them from their wrapping, opened the printed cardboard boxes and felt them roll out gently and settle in my open palm, I was in love with them—their tiny headlamps, their perfect dashboards, their impossible-not-to-fiddle-with steering wheels...

The rain held off; Toby (Lynch's dog next door) kept to their side of the yard, meaning I didn't have to hide from his long wet tongue and drooling smile. Right outside our door I played all day, down in the dirt, now with my younger brother, now on my own, driving those two cars round and round and round until I had to be carried inside to eat then carried up to bed.

The 4th of September 1968 was a Wednesday. That same week I had returned to school as a Senior Infant or Penny Baby, happy to be moving up the scale rather than bothered—as I might be now—to see newer, fresher faces lining up to take my place. The fact that I was wearing a white shirt and elasticated dickie bow made me hugely popular with the older boys in the schoolyard who could not resist snapping said apparatus every time they passed me by—a repetitive assault that would leave me with a pronounced Adam's Apple before I'd reached the age of six.

The morning gauntlet aside, however, in the afternoons I was free and back to my cars, blazing a trail in the mud and the sand and the stones of our back yard, constructing a city from nothing but movement and light.

And then one day, that Friday or some day shortly afterwards, I came in from playing and somehow left them outside.

One of those days was a visitors' day, the Sunday most probably. Our cousins from Kilkenny arrived, Orla, Rosemary and Elizabeth Ann, the two younger girls especially making the best of our labyrinthine house and out-houses, running and hiding, chasing us and being chased by us, until after dark.

Another day was a tidying day, my father pulling boxes out of one chaotic storeroom before trying to pack them back inside another.

Another day was washing day, my mother hanging nothing on one line but socks and underwear, skirts and shirts and trousers on another, so that one line danced while the other just tapped its toes…

And at last, on whichever day it was, I realised my precious cars were gone.

At night I dreamed about them. Literally. One came to get me and drove me to the hiding place of the other. A Garda rang at our door and told me he had found them in the possession of a master criminal in the Market Square. A silver spaceship landed in Main Street, just outside Dempsey's, a little green-skinned alien stepped out, waddled over, apologised profusely (or seemed to at least) and gave me back my two beloved cars.

Years passed, I stopped looking, got over the disappointment, but never to my satisfaction solved the case. Did I care? Not me, but something inside of me did.

And then in 1987 or '88, home for a weekend from Dublin I arrived at our house and, despite myself, felt my heart tighten when I was met with the sight of the builder brothers Tom and Jimmy Sullivan ("How's himself? Back with the laundry?"), digging up the shore outside the back door to clear some blockage and…

...And of course not finding anything, finding only something blocked up in me, all that time, all those years, as if I had gone home on that day to be shown that was how, even there, even then, so far on, so removed, the heart grows, the heart breaks, the heart mends...

Blinded by the Light

From the farthest reaches to just beyond the gate at the half-way point, our narrow, long back yard had a subtle incline, barely noticeable to the casual visitor but of sufficient gradient to set in motion any multi-wheeled contraption released thereon and free to move under the pull of gravity.

That gradual slope, as we discovered almost as soon as we could walk, was perfect for driving steel hoops with a stick, for learning to ride our boneshaker tricycles and bicycles (fending off the nearby walls with our palms) and, in a dramatic extension of the idea, for providing kinetic energy to the biggest and only truly communal go-kart I've ever seen: with space for ten children, half trolley-car half tank, my father's two-wheeled wooden trailer.

Kept in the upper yard where it collected pigeon droppings, cat litter and the ever-accumulating rubbish for the dump, the trailer was an enormously over-engineered monster, made from scraps and looking as if to scraps it would very soon return. The sides were rough planks, crudely bolted together; the wheels were off an earlier stripped-down car—our first Morris Minor, perhaps; the axel was the weight and thickness of a steam train piston; and the solid iron draw-bar— wherever it had come from—was a giant's or a robot's arm and quite impossible for us smaller kids to even budge.

The open eyelet in the end of the drawbar was .825 inches in diameter, or as near as makes no difference—the size of an old sixpenny piece (which is why I remember it). When I had a sixpence, for some occult reason, I almost always felt the need to double-test the measurement by dropping it through. Perhaps it was that, realising I was slowly but surely getting bigger, I needed reassurance that the world around me wasn't changing size as well.

However, this eyelet in the drawbar was a matter of some confusion to me, or rather the confusion was caused by the corresponding tow-bar on the rear of the car. For some odd reason, where one might have expected a bulbous protrusion on either one of them—over which the eyelet of the other would fit neatly to gain a hold—instead there was yet another eyelet of almost precisely the same diameter; and therefore the only way to join up car and trailer was with a stout iron pin (helmeted at the top to prevent its slipping through entirely), a manoeuvre which required the two eyelets to be perfectly aligned, and whose execution therefore sometimes vexed even the strongest of grown-ups almost to the point of rage.

That wooden trailer could make a grown man cry. How many times did I see my father or one of his part-time helpers struggling to shoulder that stiff, fixed-wheeled monster into place behind the car, inching it forward, nudging it back, only to nip his fingers painfully between the two, cursing to God, raising the pin in the air as if about to throw it but unable to do so with the wonder-filled eyes of childhood trained on him.

The fact, then, that such an untameable brute might have been sanctioned for use as a plaything is almost impossible to credit, but there it is. With the addition, some time after he first purchased it, of a small third wheel (this being on a T-shaped pole which attached somehow to the draw-bar), the previously recalcitrant trailer could now not only be directed smoothly around the yard by an unaccompanied adult, but it also became the kind of robust transport every child dreams about and of which every adult (or almost every adult) lives in fear.

Perhaps it was the fact that we were toying with such danger in a back yard we knew like the backs of our hands that seemed, somehow, to take the danger out of it.

As it was, for two or three summers (perhaps more, before I came along) my father's wooden trailer was seldom left to its self, conscripted instead to carry up to ten youngsters at a time (Borans, neighbours and various interlopers) repeatedly up and down that long back yard, all of us on our backsides on its dusty, splintery boards, unbelted, unprotected and unsecured in any way, nine of us clinging to the sides for dear life, the tenth gripping the upright steering bar which, as it hit each bump and stone and dip in turn, kicked and shuddered like a pneumatic drill.

From No. 73 next door, Carol, Des, Gwen and Shirley Robinson; Brian Lynch from No. 75, and Mary Beere, whose family at the time lived in the flat upstairs; from three doors further up Main Street, Gerard and Mary Dempsey; and from just beyond them, but being the only blonde in a brunette world, conceivably from another planet, Breda Tynan… Various others came just once (Whites, Blacks, Greys and Greenes…) but for whatever reason did not subsequently return.

The only surviving photographs of this miracle of transportation are from, I believe, 1962, the summer before I was born (though the scene is so familiar I feel I am already in the wings). Most of the usual suspects are in place, on board, crammed in tight together, ready to be set in motion by whoever will this time give the cast-off shove.

For all around that yard, of course, are adults who will lend a hand as they pass on their way, going about their serious business in that parallel universe children only ever glimpse. Down the yard there's my mother taking the washing in, breaking the air-starched sheets. Just yards away in her own kitchen doorway, Biddy Lynch is making music with a bucket of sudsy water in the outside drain. Halfway up the yard, Mick Lynch is clearing a path through a mountain of turf with a sprong (five years before the toddler Brian Foran will nickname him Rakey). And in the No. 2 loft my father is at work, nailing yet another patch of wood to the often-patched floor.

While the women are cleaning and clearing, with their head-down, head-strong stubbornness, the latter two actors—and not by coincidence of course—are clouding the air, clouding the very atmosphere with risen dust. What surprise can there be then when, only a few years from now, they will start to doubt then disregard then deny each other's point of view.

Ah neighbours: can't live with them, can't live without. When it comes, the row will be over the shared gate that leads out onto Main Street—the end of that long, magical yard, and a minor detail in the scheme of things, as it always is. But courts of law and then the silence of the grave will ensure they never manage to make up.

The gate is under Lynch's archway but four separate families have a right-of-way. Over the next few years my father will drive his commercial flat-back van through that gateway at times of his own choosing and without prior consultation with his neighbour. Mick Lynch, he will claim, often leaves the gate open at night but bolts it during the day, for no reason other than spite. At one point my father, though living in the middle of a town, will purchase a tractor and drive that too in and out through the gateway for reasons that even we, his family, find it hard to appreciate.

In November 1971 a judge will tell my father, "Mr Boran, I am beginning to think you are the unreasonable man in this case," referring to an episode in which my father has gone out and repainted red the gate which the day before Mick Lynch has painted grey.

As neighbours did, and do, Biddy Lynch has been a guest at my parents' wedding; my own godparents are Michael Jnr (Micky) and Marie Lynch. Lynchs and Borans have for years lived in two adjoining houses that were once part of a single, larger house, the blocked-up doorways in each a constant reminder. How a gateway might be allowed to divide us, after all we have known and shared together, will require another lifetime to explain.

With the death of Mick Lynch Snr. some years later, something will be laid to rest inside of my father as well. Maybe he can see that the kind of anger he has been nurturing can take him in only one direction, through the final gateway through which all mortals have to pass.

When I tell my parents I intend to go to the funeral, idealistic teenager that I am, I half expect my father to argue against it. Instead, to my surprise, he immediately declares we must all of us go, and go we do. In that moment, the reality of the scale of the falling out is clear to all of us. For the rest of her life Biddy Lynch and my father and mother are friends and good neighbours again.

But all of that is still in the future. For now there is just this intense moment of activity and, for the children recorded in the moment, this sweet potential—the only blindness caused by the brilliant sunlight of an early 1960s summer escapade.

Naked in Primary School

Memory is a fickle thing. Sometimes you look back on an event or person and, despite the original duration or intimacy, you remember scarcely anything and almost nothing for certain. And sometimes memory preserves events you're not sure happened at all, events you've lived with for so long, have recalled so often that they've become familiar friends—until one day you sit down and try to think them through and something about them refuses to make sense.

For me, one such memory has to do with one day finding myself in primary school no clothes on.

It goes like this: I am sitting in a classroom I can still see clearly, a room in Scoil Mhuire, Presentation Convent, Church Avenue, just in through the main gate and over to the left, a room I have not been inside in more than forty years but a version of which is preserved in the amber of memory.

I am five or maybe six years old. My knees are pushed together and my even-then long legs are pulled up tight beneath the desk in front of me, as if I were cold. In fact I am wearing a grey-green duffle coat, the kind with tapering lozenge-shaped buttons that must be pushed through leather eyelets and twisted to hold fast. Despite being indoors I have fastened it around me up to my neck, because below it and above my shoes and stockings, and unbeknownst to those around me, I am wearing nothing else.

Has my mother, who always comes to our bedroom in the morning to dress my younger brother and myself, somehow forgotten me? Have I slept late and jumped out of bed on the third or fourth reminder, shed my pyjamas in a heap on the floor, in a half daze grabbed my coat (where from?) and bolted for the door before anyone can stop me? Is it possible I am leaving for school without my breakfast, without my clothes, and all on my own— even if it is just down the end of a street in almost every doorway of which stands a neighbour who would watch over me, look out for me, who could address me by my surname if not my given name? Somewhere along the way could I have peed my pants and thrown them away to hide my embarrassment? Surely someone else in my family would have noticed something amiss?

Sometimes I wonder if something might have happened in the school itself? For instance, I have a half-memory of a 'game' that was sometimes played where a lone boy, a new boy, a weak boy like myself might be stripped of his pants and left in a corner while his clothes were taken back into class and, in a neat trick, ended up beneath the lid of his desk. (The narrow passage between the prefab Bantiles and the stout perimeter wall of the yard—in fact a surviving section of the 17th century fort—made it an ideal location for such assaults.)

But did it ever happen to me, or did I just worry that it might one day, a worry that took on a reality all its own?

Stranger things have happened, happened even then. Within a few years, everyone would know the names of the men we should never stop and talk to, the man who spent half of the day in the car on the hill overlooking the school, the man who would offer you a lift on the bar of his bike after pulling up to ask, "Would you have the time on you, son? Could you look after the bike for me for a minute while I go in here for a bottle of orange? Would you like a bottle yourself?" Mostly, we kids saw them coming, and the warnings of adults—obscure as they were—only confirmed suspicions we already had.

So was I ever stripped and left outside in the yard like that? I can't say for certain, but I doubt that I was. The fact that the question seems to bring with it no emotional response in any case suggests no lingering hurt. Other kids were stripped, or half- or quarter-stripped, and got to their feet crying or laughing or fighting every step of the way back, no one way to react. Perhaps I can recall it today only because it never happened at all, the threat never materialised, the danger was never present and so never passed. Perhaps what I imagine I remember is something I simply dreamed, one of those classic Freudian dreams in which the public figure finds himself outside without his clothes.

Memory is, as we know, a fickle thing. We look back and things that very likely never happened somehow continue to exert a hold on us, while things we know full well took place leave us feeling puzzled and confused.

Whatever about being naked in school, there was that day when I'd been all dressed up—short pants and braces, white shirt and dickie bow—on my first few days in Ha'penny Babies or my first week back as a Penny Baby, still learning the ropes. And when my eldest sister called to take me home, a schoolgirl just a few years older than myself, maybe running late by a minute or two, she was told by the nun who stood at the door that if she wasn't exactly on time in the future she'd lock me up inside and leave me there.

All on my own in the classroom, the entire school, Church Avenue, Portlaoise, the County of Laois, Leinster, Ireland, Europe, the northern hemisphere, the planet Earth, the Solar System, the Milky Way, the Universe, the… Perhaps, Sister, that was my weakness all along: an over-active imagination.

The Sheds

The names of the sheds and outhouses of the back yard served as reminders of the blur that just a generation before had existed between town and country. The pig shed, the chicken shed and the cow house all conjured for us the sounds and smells of a countryside that, by my time, was already a mysterious realm being slowly eaten away.

Book-ending those sheds at opposite ends of the yard were two that had securely lockable doors, and it was in these, for that reason, for a number of years at least that my father kept the heavy-duty Hessian sacks for which he was briefly the midlands distributor for the Waterford Sack and Bag Company. Stored in rolled-up, body-heavy tubes they stacked into towers, or chimneys to be more precise, for those of us who were strong yet small enough at five or six or seven or eight to scale the outsides then descend into their dark interiors, one expert footstep at a time.

And there we would stay some days for minutes though it seemed like hours (yet another adventure that centred around going unseen) before being caught and chased away by Liam Guilfoyle or some other of my father's part-time yard help, none of them much more than boys themselves.

Some of these young fellows almost literally grew up before our eyes, staying in my father's employ while he moved restlessly from distributing sacks and bags, briefly to paint, and later for the longest period to pre-made joinery, a veritable city of doors and windows and even flights of stairs that started to arrive almost every day, as it seemed, on flatbed trucks, enormous creaking, swaying loads that had to be stripped down and rebuilt inside one or other of the sheds—as if my father had been the director of some kind of museum and these huge loads were the ancient vessels he was collecting. It was, as might be expected, thirst-making work and dangerous for anyone who wasn't watching what everyone else was doing.

What we loved most, of course, was the fact that their glassless frames propped against a wall made an instant corridor or tunnel out of a new delivery, and those that were so big they had to be laid out flat on the ground were once again rooms into which we could climb and lower ourselves out of sight.

Surprising now to look back and see how few accidents there were, given the dangerous combination of an infestation of kids (and our many visiting friends) and the heavy loading and unloading that went on ceaselessly. Once in a while someone took a tumble and ran home with tears in his eyes. On one occasion a stand of fire-proof doors, stood at far too narrow an angle against a wall, toppled outwards and would surely have crushed my older brother had not a similar pile against the opposite wall now deprived it of a clear route to the ground.

Surviving the avalanches, the crushed toes, the trapped fingers and the numerous splinters, soon we were ourselves big enough to scale the fresh loads on arrival, to dismantle and rebuild those towers of windows and doors whose strange codenames—F3, G4, K6— suggested the enumerated peaks of a mountain range.

From chickens and cows to paint tins to joinery, my father's outhouses changed identities and purpose and changed our roles in them in turn. Now and then, in search of the perfect use, my father might stumble across an idea that even then (let alone in retrospect) would seem extraordinary. For a time in the late 1960s, for instance, the shed farthest away from the house became the rehearsal room for local showband The Knights, despite the fact that my father was famously hostile to most types of popular music. (This was the man who had once angrily shouted up the stairs to my sister, at the time comically mimicking an opera singer at full volume: "And another thing, turn that bloody radio off!")

Through the various incarnations, however, some of those sheds, for various reasons, avoided the brunt of my father's remodelling. Among these was the shed we called the No. 4. No doubt it was in part due to the fact that the front of it was missing, stripped away so that everything from vans to trailers to handcarts and trucks might easily be driven in. But in there against one wall (against the back wall, the only solid wall) was a stack of the ubiquitous galvanised sheets (presumably, now that I think of it, derived from the front panels of the shed itself) that had settled in no few corners of the yard.

In any case, in this instance the wedge shape they formed where they leaned against that wall was just big enough to accommodate a handful of blocks and a plank as a bench and a kid of my age (I was 6 or 7 at most), so I began to squeeze in there, an apple or banana in my pocket, my mother's and later my own Joy transistor radio in my pocket.

And maybe it was all that galvanised metal, corrugated like a wave-form, holed by nails and letting in tiny shafts of light (as if a cowboy had sauntered by and emptied his six gun in my direction), but when touched by the transistor's extendable aerial the whole construction became an aerial itself, and in there more than anywhere in our house the voices that came through the air from outside were clearer than clear and intended for me alone. In there I could follow every word as if somehow I'd climbed out of the world and into the speaker itself. *Phnom Penh, Phnom Penh.* I practised it daily, not knowing its meaning, from the tragedies of the time creating the song of myself.

The Hallowe'en Ring

On the last (or perhaps the second last) day of October 1969, I took the cheap brass ring from the Halloween brack, brought it into Sr Paula's class in the Presentation Convent Primary School, Portlaoise, and gave it to the then love of my life, the blonde beauty with the movie star name, Jacqueline Walsh. It was the innocent, instinctive gesture of a six-year old—and one for which I'd pay dearly over the next decade or more.

Though the ring had seemed to call out to me from the brack (an exposed fossil in the rock face, a lone star in its otherwise dark slice of sky), by reaching for it I had declared my hand, declared my heart and, through I hadn't realised it, sealed my fate. For we were seated around the dinner table, five siblings and our parents, and opposite me my sister and sometime archrival Mary watched with great interest. I may have declared my intentions or merely let them slip: in either case I had inadvertently made public—and given permanency to—what should have been a momentary impulse.

In the early days after my foolish romantic gesture, my mother's caution to leave the subject alone kept my sister's ribbing to a minimum. But this soon passed. And then for weeks, then months, and even years after, every time Jacqueline Kennedy Onassis was mentioned on the radio, every time Hallowe'en or rings, or anything even remotely connected, was the topic of discussion, all eyes—my sister's especially—would turn to me. And within minutes she would be chasing me through the house, upstairs and down, indoors and out, calling after me, *Jacqueline Walsh, Jacqueline Walsh,* until the former magic of that name became a torture, until the ring I'd given her (and she'd likely long since forgotten) became a link in a chain that bound me, or a noose against whose pressure I could scarcely breathe.

I recall terrible rows between my sister and myself, pointless petty arguments that would suddenly erupt into full-scale battles, and which dragged on for years: one in particular where, in a sudden fury, I threw a tea spoon across the room, luckily just missing her eye but leaving a small scar like a hook or question mark, the last time I looked, almost 40 years later, still there in miniature, still puzzling over the incident.

As the years passed, the novelty wore off, Jacqueline Walsh's name was seldom mentioned, and the names of other girls were used to tease me, or boys to tease her. But even when no name at all was spoken, the pattern was set, the threat established to linger in the air.

I often wonder now about the real reasons for those rows between us, my sister and me. Perhaps it was just because she was a girl, two years older than I was, and we were in fact competing for a position of power at the centre of the family. Perhaps it was that, for the first ten years of my life at least, I was arguably closer to my mother than to my father, and my sister, in her fated role, was working to drive the necessary wedge between us, a wedge that would force me out and away and, in a sense, help me to grow.

And what of all the wrongs I visited on her down the years, wrongs I have no doubt conveniently forgotten... What of all the seismic forces that interplay in a five-child, two-parent household that none of us could have named, being immersed and almost drowned in them? Could we unravel them even now were we to be granted sufficient leisure time and total recall?

It's more than twenty years since I've met or even seen Jacqueline Walsh. I'm not sure I'd recognize her if we were to bump into each other on the street. But if we did, what feelings, what sense of startled panic might suddenly return? Would I be able to see her for the woman she has since become, and through the eyes of the middle-aged man I myself am now? Or would I become again the six- or sixteen-year-old boy who is linked and marked—branded even—by her mellifluous name?

In the intervening years, not a single Hallowe'en has passed that I haven't thought of her, or had a thought or image of her make its way to me, like a living ghost or shade, an *aisling* figure from Irish mythology. Across the bottom of the Irish Sea in 1984 she came to find me in a squat in Brixton; up three concrete flights of stairs into my flat in Dublin's York Street in 1991, stepping over the junkies' needles on the landing; or down a whistling chimney into the unheated grandeur of my Fitzwilliam Street rooms every Hallowe'en from 1996 to 2001, conjured from air, reminding me that the past can find us anywhere.

And now I'm used to it, half expecting it—the unannounced arrival of an almost total stranger who is little more than a name, and yet bothers me still: not least for the fact that she has not aged, is still bright-eyed and beautiful while I have become darker, inside and out. And as I sense her approach up Hallowe'en stairs or down a Hallowe'en chimney, I catch myself in the mirror, for all the world like a cartoon murderer, bread-knife in hand, poised above the dome of a pristine brack that might be someone's skull or my own black heart; hoping that the bright blade of memory might once again find the glint of promised gold, or even brass, either way the liberating ring of truth.

The Empire Strikes Back

The British Empire began across the street. The residents and proprietors of what used to be Fortune's newsagents, White's grocery, The Pork Shop and Henderson's Hotel—in fact all of the business premises along that side of Main Street—whether they knew it or not had a perfect view of that once virgin territory.

Long since reclaimed from the Queen for an assortment of small back yards, bicycle sheds, outside toilets and other local wonders, in more recent times the land has been home to a VEC school and, close by, a popular discotheque where rebel sons and daughters might gather to dance (sadly not a jig or a reel) but at least on the dreams of Empire.

One hundred and four years before the Royal African Company, fifty years before the plantation of Ulster, forty-four years before the East India Company, and twenty years before the granting of a patent by Elizabeth I for the establishment of colonies in the West Indies and North America, the first plantation of the fledgling British Empire took place in Laois and Offaly, Queen's and King's counties as they came to be known.

And the first major fortification erected as part of that plantation was Fort Protector (known as Campa among the locals), later to become the market town of Maryborough, later again Portlaoise.

Among the many ironies (and a plantation town has ironies to spare) is that the town's roots in Empire are so often overlooked that until recently the only explicitly political plaque to be found in its centre was on the corner of Main Street and Railway Street, where Lewis's pub used to stand.

And God save us all (begging your pardon, Ma'am) but that was to commemorate Pádraig McLógáin, one-time National President of Sinn Féin.

History is complicated: the British Empire, I'll say it again, began across the street—if only to see if it starts to make more sense.

And Laois and Offaly were the testing grounds for the plantations of New England, Virginia, Carolina, Maryland...

It is surely fitting therefore that the opening shot in the first major insurrection of the 20th century, the first attempt to throw off British rule, should have come about just a few miles out the road.

For on Easter Sunday night, 23rd of April, 1916, the night before Irish Volunteers would move on key locations across Dublin in one of the most daring and doomed-from-the-outset acts of Irish military history, under direct orders of Patrick Pearse a contingent of Laois Volunteers (under OC Eamon Fleming of The Swan, and Vice OC Paddy Ramsbottom, Portlaoise) exploded a section of the railway line outside the town, to prevent British reinforcements from the south making their way to the capital.

No wonder the prison was a difficult subject around here.

The Safe

In the back room of my father's two-room office was an enormous safe, the kind you see in old cowboy films, often on board a train, the subject of great interest from Mexicano outlaws with their wide sombreros and droopingly comic yet somehow sinister moustaches. I don't remember that Welles Fargo was imprinted on its impossibly thick metal doors but it might well have been, and certainly any average-sized outlaw or sheriff's man could have been fitted inside of it with only the minimum of discomfort.

Where or how my father came into possession of it I cannot say. Perhaps it was there in the house before he arrived, like so much else. Or perhaps he purchased it, for whatever reason, in one of the many scrap and second-hand furniture places in Mullingar and Moate, Carlow and Tullow which he could not pass without visiting.

My father's reaction to it in some rain-swept barn would doubtlessly have been a version of his reaction to most found or stumbled-upon objects of questionable value: "Now there's a lovely little yoke I'm sure your mother will find a use for!"

The joke was, of course, that my mother, who had grown up surrounded by unwanted things, liked nothing better than the spring-clean feeling of throwing old stuff away. And while she laughed with the rest of us at her husband's hoarding and accumulating, her heart would sink at every new 'treasure' he brought home, as if scooped up in a net from the bottom of the sea or, as was the case on at least one occasion, quite literally fallen out of the sky. As on the day he returned with a giant, ragged-edged tarpaulin which turned out to be a damaged German parachute from World War II (a cluster of small holes in the middle of which we were sure were the rounds which had brought the original owner down to earth).

But if he was not entirely discriminating when it came to purchases from his favourite surplus stores and second-hand shops, my father could not have been accused of thoughtlessness when it came to taking care of those things he chose to treasure. Elaborate cleaning, folding and storing rituals were part of his ownership of a wide variety of items—from favourite blunt knives to cracked reading glasses, dried-up fountain pens and rusted flashlamps—of which special mention must be made for the way in which he routinely filed his home-made cardboard size 8 insoles in the pristine cabinets he had bought somewhere for a song.

In the long run, that safe—a cast-iron, Victorian monstrosity, fire-proof, bullet-proof and very likely resistant to TNT—being deprived of juicy secrets, dark mysteries and precious folios, ended its days as, ignominiously, a cold store before we could afford our first real fridge. Maybe 200 kilos of impregnable metal dedicated to the protection of a pound of butter, a head of lettuce and a half a dozen slices of Roscrea pork.

And, as if the waste of it had somehow hurt him, some time in the early 1970s, after our small back kitchen had finally been extended and we could now accommodate (and perhaps afford) that first real fridge, despite its magnetic, soft-shut door and automatic light (which we checked and checked and checked to distraction) my father honoured its humble predecessor by never referring to it as anything other than 'the safe'.

All Along the Watchtower

When the January 03, 1970 edition of *The Leinster Express* carried an advert for the Coliseum Cinema in Bull Lane, Portlaoise, the evening's main feature, *Hang 'em High,* appeared to promote rough justice for law-breakers.

"They made two mistakes," ran the advertising copy. "They hanged the wrong man and they didn't finish the job."

At that time, being not yet seven years of age, pretty much anything in the Coliseum Cinema was out of my reach (with the exception of supervised matinees of *Oliver, The Robe* or, the following year, *Fiddler on the Roof).* And yet the presence among us of a movie about crime and punishment can not have been lost on at least the adult population of our prison town, even if the true dominance of the gaol would not commence until its upgrading to maximum security political status two years later.

Of course, someone must have built the prison: we wondered about it even then, even as kids, passing it on our way back from Sunday walks and picnics on the Block Road, the great sturdy door and arch and walls of it a mystery even then. Especially then.

A mystery compounded by the reports my father would soon begin to read aloud at the kitchen table, within our earshot, in both the local and, increasingly, the national press. Reports of "trouble in the prison", of "protests on the Dublin Road", of "crowds from the North marching through the town". I remember hearing about attempted escapes, small-scale riots ("when lads start throwing bits of the furniture around" as an article in the same edition of the local paper puts it, life and art inextricably intertwined.

"A substantial amount of damage was done to the furniture and fittings and to the fabric of the recreational hall, in which the incident started. Items broken include two TV sets, a radio, film projection equipment and two billiard tables."

"Wow," we said in school the next day when the subject came up. "Imagine: billiard tables!"

And every youngster in the town felt torn between a life of freedom and good behaviour (but endless deprivation) and a life of crime (and punishment), the latter significantly sweetened by the presence of TV sets, film projectors and billiard tables.

Seven years later, long after the political status upgrade, another press report would list some of the games the Republican prisoners in Portlaoise were playing to help them pass the time, the same games as it happens we were playing after school: among them chess, Ludo, Snakes and Ladders and (life imitates art imitates life) a Colditz escape game.

What We Did On Our Holidays

Maybe what memory is for is precisely this: to store things away until you're old enough to understand them.

There were seven of us in all, five kids, Ma and Da. I'm thinking of a sunny day in July 1970. Ma was wearing sunglasses; Da, wherever he'd vanished to, was in a short-sleeved shirt. We'd swept the house, unplugged all the plugs, locked and bolted the front door, and now, piled into our battered old sky-blue Ford Consul, we held our breaths and waited for Da to come. There was always something about that last cup of tea before the road he found impossible to resist.

And then he came. And it was summer, perfect summer, and finally we were heading off on holiday to the fabulous, the mythical seaside town of Tramore. Triggy Mucky More, my father called it, disparagingly, but even he couldn't conceal his affection.

It was in the middle of Kilkenny city that it happened, which seems ironic now, Kilkenny being my father's native place. I think I was singing 'Ten Little Ducks' to my mother's delight and my own growing embarrassment when, without warning, like a piano from a cartoon sky, the right-hand back door of the car simply fell off iin Lower John Street, my brother almost certainly following it had it not been for my sister's quick hands.

Da applied the brake—which meant he kicked down, hard, on the middle pedal. The car stopped. And then we sat there in silence, a whole street, a whole city in silence around us, as the door of our sky blue Ford Consul shuddered to a standstill in our wake.

I'll always remember my father's terrible expression as he opened his own door, climbed out of the driver's seat and walked slowly back up the street to retrieve it, that renegade door. Infants peered at him from prams; blackbirds stared down at him from the rooftops.

But the story doesn't end there. In order to secure the door for the rest of the trip—so all of his children wouldn't all be lost along the way—my father dug a length of heavy rope from the boot and, with the door propped back in place, wound it a few times around the D-shaped inside handle. Then he played it out across the back seat to the opposite door where it was similarly wound a couple of times, pulled taut as a mooring rope and firmly knotted. To gain entry to the back seat now, we had to clamber in across and over the front.

On arrival at our rented accommodation, my brother and I made straight for the bathroom, stripped to the waist before the mirror, and spent whole wonderful minutes admiring the fading rope burns on our skin.

And what I remember is our sheer delight, and along with it a look in my father's eyes, a first glimpse of a weakness I might now call shame.

The Family that Prays Together...

We were, it surprises me to say, quite a religious family, at least when I was very young, with holy scapulars, rosary beads and various other tokens of religious observation tied around our necks, hanging on our bedroom walls or tucked away under the sheets of newspaper that invariably lined the bottoms of our clothes drawers.

I remember, for instance, one September evening, aged seven or eight, preparing to return to school after the summer holidays, and the night before, in a new pair of pants bought for the occasion, discovering a miraculous medal sewn into the waist, a medal which (notwithstanding my mother's denial) can hardly have been put there by the staff or management of Shaws (Protestant-owned if Almost Nationwide) department store.

It surprises me too to remember how long and rigorously we held to the motto 'The family that prays together stays together', though evening visits to friends' houses (where the practice was unknown) and the ever-improving quality of our television reception meant that communications from the Holy Land were finding it increasingly difficult to get through.

Back then we had a black and white Bush television, and the thing about that Bush television and, to be fair, all the valve sets of the time, was that they took an age to light up and another to fade to black again. Was there a child or adult anywhere in the world who did not at some point stand and marvel as I did at the dying television screen, at the white ball of light in the centre shrinking to a point. It was as if I were in a spaceship and, looking out the window, could see the one bright planet in the universe being slowly left behind.

The warming up, though, that was what concerned us most, especially when it came to family rosary time, for the delay was so long and the eventual start-up so unpredictable that the smartest thing to do—as we soon learned—was simply to leave it on.

Maybe we convinced ourselves that the valves could only stand so much of this now-on, now-off revision. Or maybe it was that the screen, constantly bombarded—or so we'd heard—like a kettle or cooking pot switched from hot to cold to hot repeatedly might someday fail and shatter with the strain, showering us with photons of light like so many grains of sand kicked in our faces.

Even so the decision to leave it on, in a room full of curious children, adolescents and teens, presented its own challenges for our parents, whose solution was a blue-and white-striped roller towel. Perhaps that first night my father had been carrying it over the crook of his arm, as was often the case. But even though we might all have felt a little nervous that, as we knelt and prayed, it might suddenly and spontaneously combust, by the time we finished the long Litany, the pattern had been set. All that remained over the following nights was to fine-tune the operation by trying a variety of towels, cloths and sheets (shrouds, one might say) till the right one was found.

After that it was business as usual, all of us back on our knees again, father, mother and five growing kids, turning our backs on the televised world for a few joyful, sorrowful or glorious minutes during which, out of the corners of our half-shut eyes, we struggled to unravel mysteries closer to hand: what had happened to Manolito in *The High Chapparal?* And was it true, as someone in school had claimed, that the actor who played Ironside had been seen in another programme, miraculously able to walk again?

50

The Rock of Dunamase

The great territory of Laoighis of slender swords,
Laoighis Reata, of it I speak...
  —Gilla-Neeve O'Heerin, from a topographical poem
  of Munster and Leinster, early 15th century

Given its remarkable state of disrepair, the principal attraction of the Rock of Dunamase (without doubt the best-known landmark in Laois) is the view afforded from the top of its just less than 150 ft (45 m) limestone outcrop or 'hum'.

From up there, surrounded by what looks like the abandoned building blocks of some capricious child-god (as much as a place of life and death and even slaughter), one can look out over the great territory of Laoighis—Laoighis of slender swords as it once was—and instead of distant traffic hear altogether less familiar sounds.

Perhaps with this in mind, in 1795 Sir John Parnell, Chancellor of the Irish Parliament (and an ancestor of Charles Stewart Parnell) planned to open a kind of tea-room on the top, proposing a rather handsome medieval façade to screen off those unsightly ruins. After his death, his son wisely moved on.

For as long as I can remember I've loved Dunamase, its tumbledown grandeur, its dishevelled grace. To visit it, to sit there with one's eyes closed, simply listening is to discover what I think of as the seaside of Laois—our special place to contemplate the elements.

The ruin itself consists of a watchtower and barbican gate (which at one time may, or may not, have included a drawbridge).

While history tires to make up its mind, I will go on ahead. Thus I may erect for myself a mental drawbridge and over it pass through the Inner Barbican and up to the Main Gate, set in what is known as the Curtain Wall. The Curtain Wall: imagine, a breeze might lift it, the giant stones and rocks and boulders be shaken off like so many dust motes... After this the hill rises more steeply and, with a little effort now, at last I am stood in the Upper Ward, facing what was the Great Hall and most likely the chapel.

On a good, clear day up here, it's still possible to see the soldiers about their business down below, the trails of smoke from cooking fires in the enemy camp beyond in Dysart Woods. It's possible to encounter early owner-non-occupiers like Strongbow, 2nd Earl of Pembroke and leader of the Norman invasion, going around muttering to himself, or less famous names like William de Bruce, Eve Marshall and her husband Roger Mortimer, wee hotheads like Owny Roe O'Neill and Owny MacRory O'More, men who refused, at least in the metaphorical sense, to 'know their place'.

Mostly though there are strangers up here, people wandering about in time and speaking in tongues. My classmate Danny Reddin—on an outcrop of rock dated June '77—is showing off his suntan to a host of jealous boys and admiring girls. My father and mother are eating sandwiches somewhere around the back. And a child who appears uncannily like myself is measuring the mysterious giant-steps on the north-facing side

And look, there, someone has just dropped something, a rare 9th century Egberth of Wessex coin he hasn't even noticed rolling away...

Then again it's late now. Let it lie there tonight, then for years and for decades and centuries. Some day someone will come along, find it and touch it, and all of this thing known as history will suddenly dissolve.

An Unusual Name

Is it a blessing or a curse to have an unusual name? In the Boran family mythology, for example, there are two competing theories for the history of our less-than-common surname: the first, and most likely, is that it derives from the *bodhrán* drum, and indeed the name is most densely clustered in the south midlands where bodhrán-making has long been known.

The second theory is a little more exotic, and controversial. According to *its* proponents (of whom, with a few drinks on board, I'm likely to be one), the name originates in East Africa where there's a famous Boran tribe (footnoted in Arthur Hailey's novel *Roots)* and even a distinctive, hump-backed cow of the same name. Needless to say, the Out-of-Africa theory held some appeal for my late uncle Paddy, a Missionary priest who served in Kenya for so many years that he would refer to himself, with no discernable irony, as Man from Africa. "Man from Africa is going out in the motoring car," he would say, this thick-set younger brother of my father's who must have found his occasional trips back home as baffling as he once found his new life in the Kenyan bush, a white-skinned Boran surrounded by his dark-skinned kin.

However, when weighed up against the popularity of the name in Turkey, and indeed in Thailand (where there's a city named Muang Boran), the African theory seems somewhat fanciful. Indeed, sceptics will point out that the two syllables of which our surname is composed are common in almost every language in the world.

And yet, if this is so, the almost total absence of the name in the library of English literature invites further investigation.

In Book IX of his monumental *Alfred,* the 18th century British poet and physician Richard Blackmore references a Boran (no first name given) who makes a single, brief appearance in this long and, it must be said, corpse-strewn battlefield of a poem. On this occasion, said Boran (a chief, it should be noted) is on his feet just long enough to be dispatched by the eponymous hero. Thus:

> Alfred his Weapon next at Boran threw,
> Which struck the valiant Chief, and, passing thro'
> His Bosom, enter'd deep his bleeding Heart
> That trembling felt low ebbing Life depart:
> The Warrior fell and in Convulsions lay
> Striving with earnest Eyes to catch the Day.

There's something almost touching about this set piece that leaves my namesake so cruelly dispatched (the victim of the 18th century equivalent of a drive-by shooting). Certainly, it's a pity that there's no other reference to who this particular Chief might have been—the inventor of the much too popular *bodhrán,* I'm tempted to suggest.

Perhaps it was the style of the epic poems of the early 18th century to distinguish minor characters with names if only to flesh them out before cutting them down. Either way the first appearance of a Boran in English letters is a less than distinguished one.

And, it must be admitted, some two hundred and fifty years later, the same may be said of the second.

In Christopher Logue's *War Music**, the scene this time is Troy, the city made famous by Homer (and, incidentally, widely believed to have been in northwest Turkey). Some way into this action-packed retelling of *The Iliad,* Logue's Boran, again without a given name, gets *his* walk-on part, *his* fifteen seconds of fame:

> Hector is in the armour. Boran lifts
> A coiling oxhorn to his lips. And though
> Its summons bumps the tower where Priam sits
> Beside a lip that slides

Out of a stone lion's mouth into a pool,
The king is old and deaf, and does not move.

In other words, on this occasion after waiting a quarter of a millennium for a second shot at literary immortality, like Joshua at the walls of Jericho Boran emerges from the shadows to blow his horn, but... what he blows with such conviction falls on deaf ears.

So much for ancient Britons, Greeks and Turks— gone, every one, the way of Man from Africa.

And yet our names must come from somewhere, must have a place and moment of conception, and in the current of our lives must attach to something. Do our names become us, or do we become our names? What if the immigrant families of recent years are carrying the names that will be seen as typically Irish in centuries to come? The Nagys from Naas perhaps, Kowalskis from Castlecomer; the Piotrowskis from Main Street, Portlaoise.

And when it comes to the name Boran, that familiar mystery, it was my father who beat the rest of us hands down, Richard Blackmore's, Christopher Logue's, and all my own pseudo-literary efforts rolled into one. For, faced with the task of finding a name for his 1970s small-town travel agency, at first he flirted with the craziest of ideas: Sky Boran, Wind Boran (which reduced us kids to tears of laughter, for obvious reasons) and even Hawk Boran, a name better suited to a 9th century Saxon overlord in the Blackmore vein. A single leaf of Basildon Bond writing paper preserved his initial brainstorming session for decades in a cupboard, until it, then the cupboard, then the business and building itself went the way of all things.

Even so, the final item on that list survived them all as if, by whatever magic, my father had come face-to-face with the name he would choose, the name that had chosen him.

For whether by accident or miracle, in a nod to transience and the impermanent, to the movement of peoples across the planet and through time, on the last line of that page my father accepted his Fate, his Destiny. And I see him still, in a light blue shirt and brown check jacket, one Saturday morning out there on Main Street, admiring his newly-painted signboard which reads— inevitably in retrospect—not just plain *Boran* but *Airboran* Travel.

Camera Obscura

At some point our house and the houses on either side had been one enormous building, the division into first two and then, more than fifty years later, into three separate houses leaving a host of odd architectural features in the middle one, the one in which we lived.

As well as the staircases that lead from the first floor landing to single rooms on the floor above—and doorways that lead nowhere at all—there was the bedroom I shared with my brother, this top-floor, narrow, even somehow elongated room which seemed to have been cut in half then interrupted with a massive chimney breast so that its one low window at the front looked like an afterthought.

It was not, however, just the form of the room but its position above the street—north facing, always in shade, and overlooking the large shop-windows opposite—that helped to give it its remarkable quality.

On Saturday mornings, when my brother and I would lie on in bed, talking, half dreaming, maybe reading or listening to the radio, through the gap above the curtains would come a narrow beam of light—for all the world like the beam of light that strikes a cinema screen.

In truth, we were sleeping in a classic *camera obscura,* the dark room from which the camera takes its name. No one had designed it: it was simply there. It was as if, most bright mornings, someone was outside our window, hovering there, three floors up, projecting images deep inside our room. And as we lay there in our beds on opposite sides, what we saw on the ceiling overhead was every car and every pedestrian who passed down below, the precision of the image determined by the intensity of sunlight, itself determined by the weather, the time of year, the time of day.

On a day when all the elements conspired we could easily make out the colours and shapes of the cars below and, with a little concentration, the general form (and therefore the gender) of the pedestrians, guessing their identities from the progress of a sprightly walk or the distorted outline of a bicycle drawn above our heads.

Had we knocked it down and started again with the aim of improving the reception, or of simply duplicating the desired effect in another room, we would doubtless have failed. For whatever accident had given it to us, this Main Street movie house had been just that and would not be easily reproduced.

Camera obscura, the dark room. It is 1969 or 1970 or 1971... Years from now my brother will become a photographer, often employing projection of one kind or another in his images. When I grow up I will write stories, poems, maybe some songs. For now, all I can do is lie here and watch, rubbing my eyes, pinching myself at my good luck. "Look at that one: that's Mick Whelan crossing the street..."

Time spent lazing in bed is time well spent.

The Garden

As town gardens go, the garden of 74 Main Street was enormous. Laid out originally by my mother's Aunt Kit, it boasted the twin attractions of both wild and tended plots, gathered roughly at opposite ends like a metaphor for the town/countryside divide on which we then lived. Rose bushes, a small orchard, even a small vegetable patch: the garden had it all. And grass that grew so tall a child might be lost inside it for days...

Accessed through a large gate at the town end of our yard, on first entering it the garden looked like a relatively unkempt field of about half an acre, a little piece of the countryside surviving at the rear of the town. But while the point of entry might have suggested wildness, once entered into (with all the connotations there of a bargain or spiritual tryst), the garden's true nature revealed itself.

In an era when black and white newspapers and black and white television had not really prepared us for it, the first thing one noticed was colour. Built up to a height of maybe eight feet from large, limestone rocks, the wall that divided the garden from the back yards of our neighbours the Finnamores, the Bennetts and the other Main Street residents was a veritable riot of colour: roses trained up the pitted wall in red and pink and white detonations; laburnum, lilac and buddleia beyond and reaching through each other; staked out at one end the vegetable plot of carrots, potatoes and peas in their pods; and, my favourite spot, the dappled shade and swing-honouring stillness beneath the apple trees.

Civilization, it seems undeniable, grew up with and depended on gardens, and in the garden of 74 Main Street it was so easy to see how it had come to pass. And yet, for all the sense of elegant control the garden exuded (at one end at least), it was the other end we were often drawn to as kids, that long, wind-blown grass which, in the days before electric or petrol lawnmowers, could only be brought down to size by my father, his sleeves rolled up, a handkerchief hanging from his back pocket as he wielded that most medieval of implements, the full-length scythe.

"Stand well back now," he'd warn us, even before he came out of the No. 6 shed, the scythe slung over one shoulder, its smooth twisted shaft thick as a python, the gleam of a warrior's broadsword off its tapered blade.

And for all its suggestion of the Spanish Inquisition or the Grim Reaper, that scythe somehow bestowed on my father an almost classical ease and poise and deftness. It turned a man who could struggle with a shoelace or a typewriter ribbon into a dancer, however foreboding his expression might have been to keep us at a respectful distance.

That garden must have been a blessing to both of my parents. For my mother, it was the town garden her aunt had painted, quite beautifully, and whose image hung in a gold-leafed frame on the wall of our sitting room, like a reminder of what our weekday, work-a-day lives are offered up for. For my father, it was a small vegetable plot some 20 miles from the farm where he'd grown up, a place to recreate and re-ignite the magic of life and cultivation.

But it was that yearly stepping-out into the long grass, scythe across his shoulder, that seemed to give him his greatest sense of purpose—watched, as he was, by his three small boys and two small girls, and his own child self, and the shades of his father and his father's father before him, all of them stepping out alongside him to observe the ritual.

When my father first came to Portlaoise, and 'married in' to that house, he knew nothing about gardens, whatever about vegetables, so there must have been days when the likelihood of their tending to both the aged and decrepit 11-room house, and now a garden straining at the leash, seemed slim at best. And yet with five young children to occupy their time—and undo their best efforts—they kept that garden alive, struggling to recreate the picture Aunt Kitt had painted of it, like a kind of challenge to my mother and the generations that would follow.

In the event, the garden survived until 1970, in which year Laois County Council placed a Compulsory Purchase Order on it—or on my parents as they felt the blow to have been aimed—before driving a four-lane town bypass through the heart of it. Such is change. Such is progress. Once a kind of Eden, full of butterflies and birdlife, rabbits even, foxes no doubt, in no time the garden, and Dunne's and all the other surrounding fields, became instead an unlevelled, half-gravelled and badly tarmacked car park, pock-marked and blistering in the sun, overflowing when it rained. A black, hard-underfoot and huge expanse of emptiness, on which, in the late evenings, when the cars had all moved off, leaving only take-away wrappings and cigarette ends, my younger brother and I would explore, feeling a strange pull as we crossed the invisible lines where once the garden had ended and the world began.

And now the garden is, truly, ended—in another meaning of the phrase—and a new world has taken its place. Our privilege of having such a treasure to enjoy has been measured against the needs of a growing town. But all is not lost. There is still Aunt Kitt's painting, a vestigial memory of a sacred garden hanging on my mother's wall. And even today, when I have occasion to go back, sometimes I walk through that car park to stand in a queue at the bank ATM almost on the very spot where my mother's roses, her Aunt Kitt's roses, rambled and ranged, made purchase and counter-claim, and, in a tiny crumbling hollow of which, almost 40 years ago already, I see again my first-ever miracle: the new emerging from the old; in a weave of twigs and sticks and useless things, a pair of blue-grey, light-washed and fragile, yet unexpectedly resilient (in memory at least) nest eggs.

Hand-to-Hand Combat

I am down on my belly, my nose about half an inch above the gravel, bullets whizzing inches above my head, the barbed wire of bindweed and twigs blocking my way to the enemy bunker in the doorway of the No.2 shed.

Since the garden and fields were dug up to build the James Fintan Lalor Avenue, the churned-up piles of dried-out mud have proven the perfect ammunition for enacting war games: fist-sized and portable, exploding on impact in a spray of fine clay and gravel, and as a bonus leaving an impact mark precisely like that of a shell.

Suddenly it falls quiet. Perhaps they are reloading. But in the five- or ten-second break I have a length of old wood thrown down across the barbed wire and in a hail of anti-personnel clay bombs I'm over the bridge above a burning river of fuel, zigzagging through gun fire, dodging in and out of doorways, a technique I've improved by watching British troops in the north on television.

And though separated from my unit now, I've made it on my own, a grazed wing and shrapnel wound above my thigh scarcely slowing me down.

And then I'm in the door, a stun grenade thrown ahead of me, following without thought for my own safety to mop it up, to clear it out, shouting, "Hands up! Hands above your heads, you swine!" brandishing my Lee Enfield hurley or my Sten gun tennis racquet with (unbeknownst to them) the jammed firing pin.

And later, after marching out my prisoners, after handing them over to the waiting guards who are grateful to have someone like me to do their dirty work, even in their moment of defeat I show my enemies some respect, stopping to salute their commanding officer.

"Captain."

"What about ye." he says. "Now where's them billiard tables we heard talk of? And what are we meant to do for cigarettes?"

And then the setting sun tells me teatime beckons and I'm running down the yard back to the house.

The Housewife's Choice

Mrs X had a problem with her bunions. I was in Gannon's chemists sent there by my mother for a bottle of Benilyn Expectorant or a childproof tub of one-a-day Haliborange (among the few medicines that were always in the cupboard above our sink).

In the queue on this occasion I found myself behind the wide-hipped, Wellington-booted, dun-coated figure of Mrs X, a woman whose name I never knew but would have recognised even from a distance by the distinctive stop-start motion of her progress which gave her the appearance of a hesitant stranger in the town, a child who had strayed in from the dark woods, or an escaped prisoner trailing ball and chain.

On this particular day I was closer to her than ever, close enough to smell the countryside off her clothes—the feed, the flowers, the taste of earth itself. I saw her large almost masculine hands fumble with the clasp on her purse, count out one-pound notes as though she were at a mart, flattening them down on the counter as if on the hood of a car. Whatever bunions were she was "crippled with them, wore out with them," she said, and I had the impression that she would pay anything to know as little of them as I did, an eavesdropping kid in plimsolls who danced through the street as if barely touching the ground.

A pocket dictionary at home had nothing to say of bunions (was I spelling it correctly?) but the rhyme with onions made me wonder if the thing that was growing on the feet of Mrs X (I had followed the conversation with the chemist, to a point) was not some kind of vegetable. I kept thinking of what a teacher had once said about one of the kids in my class that there was so much dirt behind his ears she could have sown potatoes. Mrs X had onions growing in her shoes? No wonder she had trouble getting around!

Weeks or even months later I found myself beside Mrs X again, this time in Whelan's butchers a few doors up, me on another errand for my mother. "Young Boran there," said the Mockler with a grin, at once letting me know he'd spotted me and gently cautioning me to wait my turn.

Mrs X was watching closely while he did his stuff, holding up and showing the front and then the back of a cut of steak ("the finest bit of *mate* you'll find anywhere, missus") while his sister Eilie waited by his side to wrap.

My thumb testing the tip of the meat hook that protruded from beside the doorjamb, ready to display a fine dead beast (slaughtered out the back by the Mockler himself), I happily watched from the door. All the while Mrs X's eyes moved back and forth between the steak in his hand and the question marks of half a dozen chops laid out on a tray behind.

When she finally settled on the steak, it was only because the choice had already been made for Mrs X and, almost without looking now, she reached over and accepted the book-thick slab, already oozing a red shadow of blood through the paper in which it had been wrapped and tied with string.

Throughout the transaction Mrs X scarcely spoke. Silence between adults and kids wasn't unusual, but between adults and other adults, and between adults out shopping, it certainly was. Here was a woman, I thought, who one day knows exactly what she needs—ointment for bunions—and the next day can't make up her mind. Was that what it was like to be "afflicted"?

If so it was a feeling I knew only too well. For already I had spent hours and hours of my short life (if all the minutes were to be added up) in front of the glass displays in Ger Brown's shop up the street, tantalised by Pink Panther bars and Sweet Cigarettes, Love Hearts and Macaroons—only to arrive back home ten minutes later, empty-handed, foot-sore and head-staggered by too much choice.

Answering Back

Strange to think that one's neighbours might once have provided all the necessary goods and supplies, often across a counter right there in their own houses, their own premises. But so it was, for centuries, in towns like ours.

Not that it was all plain sale-ing, as it were. People could be suspicious of neighbour-traders, inevitably wondering if the need to produce a small profit was not at times an obstacle to friendship. As long ago as 1833 a report of the Municipal Enquiry Commission found significant problems with certain aspects of trade within the town of Maryborough and voiced its concerns in language that hinted at conspiracy.

"The internal regulations of the town are deplorably bad," the report held. "False weights and measures are in general use, by which all classes, and particularly the poor, suffer severely." To be fair, such imbalances were not unique to Maryborough.

It must also be said that a life in the service, and under the scrutiny, of the public is not for everyone, and there have been many who found themselves behind counters who might have been better employed (or unemployed) elsewhere.

On his bad days my father was certainly one of these. At least by the time we kids were on the scene, banging and roaring about in the background, he had long since taken on the appearance of a man who might have preferred to be almost anywhere else. After some dealings with one particularly hard-to-please customer (was he from Hazelhatch, Co. Kildare?), my father afterwards referred to every troublesome customer as "a bloody hazelhatcher", "a blithering, blistering ramlatcher" and so on through a multitude of permutations, the more difficult to enunciate the better.

In Fortune's newsagents across the street, meanwhile, Sadie Fitzpatrick leaned in the opposite direction, towards silence, or at least restraint, being seen to bite her lip when my brother Peter came in on his weekly quest for comic books, her loving arrangement of the latest arrivals—spread out and overlapping like a deck of cards on the counter—meaning nothing before his grubby little hands.

But the best put-downs or jibes or barbs were reserved for customers, not because they were always right, but because, like expert comedians, they knew to exit following their best lines.

And so it was that our family friend and neighbour Christy Foran, a perennially good-humoured, upbeat man (and the father of my school pal, Martin) one day went to buy a bottle of milk in a Main Street shop with a famously bad-humoured assistant. Even as kids, when this was the only place to stock our favourite brand of salted nuts, it was a constant dilemma whether to face the music or go without.

On the day in question, probably whistling to himself as was his habit, the bold Christy duly sauntered in, plucked up a glass milk bottle from a tower of crates in the centre of the floor and, not unreasonably in those pre-refrigerator days, enquired:

"Is this today's milk?"

"What did you think it was?" came the sour reply.

"Ah," says Christy, "I thought it might be tomorrow's."

Middle Eastern Influence

In the archway, and against the front window-ledge, of Ramsbottom's public house on Lower Main Street (separated from Main Street proper by an almost imperceptible turning of maybe 15 degrees), for at least a decade and possibly more stood a man who was only ever know to us as the Arab Shea.

For years I wasn't even sure if others in the town called him that, if he might have been offended by it (if he was *meant* to be offended by it), or precisely how the name had come about. Maybe it was just our family's name for him and dated back to the days when I was still holding my mother's hand as we passed him on the way to Sunday mass or down to collect a square of Woods' brown bread in Marie Dunne's.

On all of these occasions, no matter if we greeted him or not, he'd look on with a strangely distracted air, like a man who continued to find the town as confusing as the day, maybe 50 years before, he'd first come into it in tears.

Right up to the time I was trailing home from discos late at night, in a crowd of friends or, more often than not, alone (though once in a while with a girlfriend's smaller hand in mine), the Arab manned his lonely post and never gave me or anyone I know the slightest bother. Now and then, to be sure, he put out a hand to bid me to stop and asked me a question I didn't entirely understand, but took no offence whatsoever when I offered him something of which he might or might not have been in need. Sometimes it might be difficult to tell.

The other Arabs I recall meeting in Portlaoise in my childhood were *real* Arabs, from Saudi Arabia, as it happens, and the most extraordinary visitation we might have witnessed short of the Second Coming or one of my older brother's UFOs finally turning up. Brought to the town by the ESB for training in the summer of 1971 or '72, they stayed only about a week but in that short week changed the complexion of a place we thought we knew.

On the particular afternoon we first met them, we'd been out on our bicycles doing a 'round of the block' of the Abbeyleix, Meelick and Timahoe roads, had come back over the new 4-lane bypass and now, in a small patch of green that had yet to be dug up for car-parking spaces, were casually kicking a ball around. Suddenly we found ourselves approached by five or six unusually skinny, I remember noticing, dark-skinned men: all in their mid 20s, lively, laughing, loud, they negotiated by pointing, clapping us on the shoulders, and then they joined us in the most exciting game of soccer there ever was.

Ahmed and Ali, Mohammed and maybe a Mustapha... The names of the others I have since let get away, but the impression their appearance made on me was enormous. Saudi Arabia: all I knew about it was where it was, approximately, on the world map on my bedroom wall: a huge stretch of sand that bordered the Red Sea. Wasn't that where—or approximately where—Aladdin had come from? Which made it seem then like an even stranger vision: to play football in a patch of grass that, before the bypass, had been our garden, and with a handful of men from a fairytale land of caves and camels, scimitars and sultans, mirages and magic lamps.

The Arab Shea, it turns out, was known to almost everyone, one of those 'characters' every small-town population needs and recognises but never knows much about. He had earned the name, I am told, after featuring in a St Patrick's Day parade many years before, wearing some kind of vaguely middle eastern headdress, an innocent nod, no doubt, to the Arabian Nights.

Strangest of all, perhaps, was that the site of that international playing field—"Ahmed, over here! Mohammed, come on, pass it on!"—with the next blink of my eyes would become (cue servant girls in exotic uniforms, impossibly luxurious goods, flickering lamps and whispering music overhead) the town's first really full-scale supermarket, a veritable (what else to call it?) Aladdin's Cave.

The Cut

A mountainside crowned with spruce and pine; after the familiar sequence of hills and fields, the stop at the little shop at the turn for Coolrain, Golly Bars and assorted ice-creams dripping down our sleeves as we remount and drive away; after the slow rise up out of the low bogland into higher bog then the opening out of the road into the landscape of Slieve Bloom, the road curving round, and up, and up, and round and down at last into Monicknew, 'The Cut' as it is to us.

Sunday after Sunday of my childhood, this is where we come, to the small stone-surfaced car park and wooden picnic seats which are, we like to imagine, the last sign of civilization before the deep, dark woods. Out here, like Fionn and Oisín, the Virginian and Trampas, Hannibal Heyes and Kid Curry—"the two most successful outlaws in the history of the west"—or whatever other heroes hold our imaginations at the time, we wave goodbye to uninterrupted daylight and head out along the wilderness trail, with only the flow of the river to help us find our way.

The flow and churning rapids of the Glen River. The first small solid pine-log footbridge crosses an unfathomable gorge, on the opposite side of which, among the dappled ferns, the occasional burst of wild clematis and a dozen other tiny flecks of coloured light for which we have no names (being from elsewhere) we discover our parents, side by side, in the partial shade: our mother, seated, reading the *Sunday Independent*, our father stood beside her in a short-sleeved shirt, a transistor held to his one good ear and a gaze that says he too is reaching out, out, out into a parrallel world.

"And there's a capacity attendance today at Croke Park for this year's All-Ireland Senior Hurling Final between—"

The reception goes and comes and comes and goes.

One sunny Sunday we drive to Thomastown, I think it is, to hear a speech by someone named Erskine Childers; once in a while we visit my mother's sisters in Roscrea, coming home with armfuls of fresh rhubarb, wrapped in newspaper, and boxes of sweets they buy in the local Cash & Carry, wholesale. Some Sundays we go nowhere, screening out the rain with a newly-borrowed library book or whatever cowboy movie or family musical RTÉ has decided to show. Once in a while we stroll in the gardens at Ballinakill or Abbeyleix. But most Sundays we spend like this, charging along on the forest path close to the Glen River, watching our parents in silence from the depths of the wood.

Though every first Sunday in September is significant, generally being the last day before we go back to school, this particular Sunday, September 4th 1971, is especially memorable, preserved for me now, stored and dated like a home-made jam or a photograph of a hazy family outing on which somewhere has afterwards added the provocation of detail.

For today is not only my 8th birthday (and we are spending it in my favourite place), but it is also the day of the All-Ireland Senior Hurling Final which this year pits Kilkenny against Tipperary, my father's against my mother's home county, in a contest Tipperary will go on to win.

"A Clash and a smash of the ash…" reads the caption to a photo on the front of the following morning's *Irish Times*, while the headline, '61,000 see Tipperary Beat Kilkenny' will do little to make my father's disappointment easier to bear. That there are a mere 3 points in it is small consolation. With two goals and eleven points under his belt, Kilkenny's Eddie Keher yet again excels himself and gives my father his only moments of good cheer.

Mostly it is "the bare-footed wonder with the ball now", as Micheal O'Hehir sings the progress of the Tipp captain Babs

Keating, like a god descended temporarily to earth, playing much of the spellbinding game in his bare feet.

Later that afternoon, heading back to the car, maybe on the same path as Fionn MacCumhaill once trod, either when hiding out up here from Goll or One-Eyed MacMorna (the warrior who first killed his father and later his son), or when he and the entire Fianna came up here to train, hurleys at the ready, no doubt, like the weapons they so obviously are, in deference to my wounded father following quietly behind I try not to let my feet make a single sound.

'Hey Jude'

"Paddy Boran is no good, chop him up for fire and wood. If he doesn't do for that, give him to the pussy cat!"

Hard to credit it now, but there was a time when those words, sing-songed in the side-yard of the Presentation Convent, were like all of the slings and arrows of outrageous fortune being loosed at once in my direction.

"Sticks and stones will break my bones, but names will never hurt me." This, of course, was the stock reply, the collective magic by which the downtrodden attempted to get themselves back on their feet.

To a great extent, however, the oppressed learn to keep their mouths shut and to cultivate invisibility. Indeed, certain periods of childhood might fairly be described as tugs-of-war between the contradictory instincts to sing out the song of the self, on the one hand, and to merge into the background, on the other.

In my time at school some lads were better at it than others, moving from background child to middle or foreground adolescent with apparent ease. Others seemed continually to stagger under the weight of every public utterance, and to shrink and cower in those times when words failed them.

My school friend Martin Foran was not one of these.

When my age could still be written with a single digit, Martin Foran was my best friend. He was also, for a number of years, my next-door neighbour, his parents living in a small flat over Lynch's house in No. 75, so that we quickly became inseparable pals. Foran & Boran: we sounded like a law firm but probably acted more like little criminals, running wild in our shared back yard, climbing into the even-then dangerously dilapidated sheds that seemed to stretch all the way out to where the town ended and the fields of grazing, dreaming cattle began.

Martin was not afraid of his own voice and as a small kid he wasn't shy to make pronouncements on the way he found the world. When another local youngster proved a little slow to enunciate with the clarity adults and other kids expect, the diminutive Martin one day declared, to my mother's delight, tht Michael L___ "talks rale quare".

But there was no censure in my mother's amusement, or indeed in the young Martin's observation, however crudely he might have phrased it. In a sense, both might be said to have been recognitions, even celebrations, of difference. In those apparently homogenous, cut-off small-town times, a child from around the corner or up the street was like a being from another world, and the observations of children like Martin at least recognised those essential differences.

Private P Foran (3235). It's one of the names of the 177 officers and men of the 4th Battalion (Leinster), Queen's County Regiment who died in action in the First World War, commemorated on the War Memorial that back then still stood in Bank Place and has since been removed a half kilometre east out of the path of increasing traffic.

In the early 1970s, walking to the Railway Station with our mother to take the train to Dublin (off to the zoo or the Panto at the Gaiety), we'd run on ahead to trace the immortalised names with our fingers while she caught up with us then stood there thinking quietly to herself, about what exactly we never understood. I remember being impressed by the vague idea that someone with my best friend's name had died fighting for our freedom. In my mind's eye, it was as if the 4th Battalion Leinster Regiment had been standing out on the Abbeyleix Road, a solid wall of flesh just beyond the sign that read 'Welcome to Portlaoise', and from which vantage point they had undoubtedly fired into the hordes of German troops who, for whatever reason, had been threatening the town.

At some point most kids experiment with a trick to test the boundary between being heard and unheard, seen and unseen. The quietest teens don the gothic uniform and wait to see what the chosen part might bring.

My school friend Andy Dunne, having what's now called a play-date in our house one afternoon, tested the boundaries in his own inimitable style. While my mother served up a feed of sausages and beans, clutching his chest young Andy suddenly fell to the kitchen floor, howling "Cancer! Cancer!"—a performance we kids thought the best thing we'd ever seen and which even the adults present would long afterwards recall.

Other kids howled for attention, but missed the essential extra ingredient of humour. Others called each other names, used words like a kind of weapon instead of a tool for liberation. One or two came up with something new, wholly their own, unique among the linguistic keys by which one might escape one old identity and expand into the next.

My friend Martin's trick was unique. A teenager now, suddenly, strolling up Main Street with his distinctive cock-of-the-walk swagger, arms swinging freely by his sides, without the slightest warning he'd suddenly roar out at the top of his voice, *"Hey——"* (causing the population of the entire street—school kids, shoppers, members of the Garda, assorted passers-by—suddenly to turn round to see who might be calling them; after which delay our hero would blithely continue, as if all along singing to himself) "Jude—don't make it bad…" and then resume his passage through the town, alive as a youngster can hope to be, and scarcely able to contain his delight in being.

Perfume: A Christmas Story

The scents of cinnamon and cloves; of parsley and thyme and basting turkey breast; of sputtering candles and half-drunk glasses of sherry; of the heady pine fresh smell of the Christmas tree; of the sulphurous bite of freshly-fired cap guns; of the citrus tang of a pyramid or my father's beloved oranges in the bottom of a kitchen cupboard, intensified by having been left undisturbed for days. And, after dark, the gritty aromatic blend of fog and turf smoke hanging over the town, over the entire countryside, allowing those who closed their eyes to imagine it was not just years but centuries that had passed, and that they, and we, were the first settlers in this part of the country, the first Christians huddled around a fire, gathered before a manger.

Christmas in my childhood would never have been complete without such smells, such scents, such transporting bouquets, aromas and fragrances. And so it should come as no surprise that the thing that changed Christmas for me forever was not the rumour that Santa Claus did not exist but a revelation that had to do with perfume.

What happened was that, as usual, my younger brother Michael and myself were trying to get the presents for the rest of the family out of the way so we could go back to the real business of Christmas: listening, hinting, spying and speculating. In our big rambling house on Main Street, we were, for all the world, like Rosencrantz and Gildernstern in Shakespeare's *Hamlet*, hiding in the shadows and the wings, trying to piece together the plot from half-heard lines, hints and fragments. Christmas morning would doubtless bring an end to our misery, and the revelation of our own new possessions but, in the meantime, finding something for both our mother and eldest sister Margaret was, as ever, proving next to impossible. Our once-yearly visit to the Ladies Department of Shaws had left us little short of traumatised: a gauntlet of strange items of underwear to be run through, at the end of which the inevitable disappointment of homely tea towels, calendars and predictable gift vouchers.

The usual litany of possibilities had, of course, been gone through—A book? But what book? A record? But which one?—until finally we wondered if there might not be something to be discovered in the new supermarket which, not long before, had opened right behind our house, and down whose long, brightly lit and spacious aisles we soon found ourselves wandering, like babes in the woods, small change jingling in our hands.

I don't remember which one of us spotted them first, and had the idea—it's a long time ago now, so I'll blame my brother—but two minutes after seeing the most amazing special offer on selected perfumes, we were being processed through the check-out by a girl with tinsel in her hair, our four purchases (two each for my mother and sister) clinking together in what might reasonably have been described as a festive mood.

Even wrapping those particular gifts was easier than wrapping the bits and pieces we'd gotten for the other members of the family, partly because all four were the same, and partly because what we learned wrapping my sister's could be quickly applied to the wrapping of my mother's. We were, my brother and I, a conveyor belt operation before we even knew the meaning of the phrase, one folding the reindeer and plum pudding wrapping paper, the other standing by with patterned Sellotape and scissors.

As luck would have it, and just as we finished wrapping her own two gifts, my sister walked in on our preparations. And though we managed to hide them behind our backs, we felt we had no choice but to come clean on what we'd bought for our mother.

"Perfume," we said excitedly. "We got Ma perfume," hugely pleased with ourselves but a little nervous of giving the game away.

"Oh, lads…" said our sister, looking at the gifts, her smile, we should have noticed then, a little too large, her eyes a little too bright, as if some old joke had suddenly come into her mind unbidden. With nothing more to be said on the subject, she gently ruffled our hair and left the room, and we worked on, in concentrated silence, efficient as a pair of Santa's elves.

Christmas morning, we realised our mistake. Having dealt with the usual scarf and gloves from various family members, a second copy of Gay Byrne's *To Whom It Concerns* which one of her own sisters had already unwittingly given her the year before, our mother tore the paper from the gift we'd lovingly wrapped the evening before and, "Oh—" her voice just seemed to hover in mid air.

For a second she looked at Margaret and Margaret looked at her as if they were both trying to judge the best way to proceed. And then both of them, as one, began to laugh. Gently at first. And my brother and I laughed too (albeit a little uncomfortable still, not really sure about what was going on). And we were joined then by my other sister and other brother, and presently by my father who, a glass of white wine in his hand, had come upstairs to see what all the laughter was about.

But it couldn't have made a whole lot of sense to him to find that the object of our hilarity was not just one, or two, or three, but four individual aerosol cans of what my brother and I at last now knew was not cheap perfume but very cheap deodorant stood there in the centre of the floor.

Yet even now, so far on, it is difficult to trace how moments like that can change from being moments you cringe about for years to being the very moments you would pay almost anything to suffer through again.

Take the Money and Run

One of my favourites of the old pictures that survived for decades in 74 Main Street was a print of a group of men (beggars, or off-duty soliders perhaps) seated around a table, playing cards. Unbeknownst to the others, under the cover of the table the man on the left was passing a card to the one on the right, gripping it between the toes of his bare foot.

Public houses often have prints of the sort, the men for the most part replaced by foxes or dogs or occasionally pigs. In a time still not too distant they made up a sub-genre of art subjects as popular as, in the 70s, weeping children, bowls of waxy apples and pierrots brandishing guitars.

Before the advent of television, such images were the equivalent of the popular adverts where monkeys act out strikingly human scenarios, often with comical or downright disastrous results. People could laugh at each other, and occasionally at themselves, by pointing and laughing at such images. Who cared that foxes, being colour-blind, could hardly enjoy snooker, or that dogs would make hopeless card players given that at every decent hand their wagging tails would give the game away.

And as for pigs, well they were funny just standing there, like a certain kind of adult who takes himself too seriously.

Having an image of this sort in such a prominent place in my childhood causes me to wonder now what its effect might have been on me, and whether it might relate to an event in the early 70s, the connection with which I have never really considered until now.

We were on holiday, as we so often seemed to be, in Tramore, Co. Waterford, a seaside town of hills and cannon guns; of once grand hotels fallen on hard times; of a man-made lake with yellow-and-white pedal boats on top, and the shell of a plane we told ourselves was the Red Baron's on an island in its centre. Tramore of the nearby Metal Man statue and the wonderful 3-mile strand, each year remarked upon by my mother who felt the need, like Wordsworth in 'Tintern Abbey', to mark in words both our return and the passing of time.

Tramore was also, for us kids at least, the world of candyfloss and toffee apples, of bumper cars and waltzers, of one-armed-bandits and a variety of other coin- and slot machines, gulping and churning, tinkling and very occasionally dribbling as one walked past them, the flash of their fruit-coloured eyes an impossible come-on for a small town boy like me.

Especially like me. For so enamoured was I of these money-shifting androids, these cash-counting automatons that, following a previous holiday, halfway up our back yard in a pile of old sand I had constructed my own Gambling Harrada (arcade meets harem?), under whose flimsy galvanized roof and armed with nothing more than a 12-inch ruler I would mimic (Las Vegas style) the spellbinding movements of an assortment of gaming machines thereby to seduce my brothers and sisters to drop or roll or toss or flip or otherwise part with their hard-earned loot in half a dozen 'try your luck' games that each delivered it expressly to my pocket.

At the Tramore 'Amusements' therefore, I was beside myself.

On this particular day I imagined I was feeling lucky and, having effected, yet again, to stray away from the family group in the nearby dodgem zone, I found myself alone before a tantalizing stack of pennies, a robotic arm moving back and forth behind it somehow (surprise, surprise) never managing to connect.

Perhaps I helped it or intended to do so. Perhaps, because the most recently added three or four or five of those pennies were still warm with the heat of my fist and of the pocket of my pants, I felt

I had a claim on that tower, like the mountaineer who, though the hazardous journey has just begun, already sees himself arriving at the summit.

Either way, whatever exactly transpired (and certainly before at least the metaphorical penny had dropped), thirty seconds later I found myself in a dimly-lit room, surrounded by cardboard boxes, rolls of cable, stackable chairs, and face to face with the middle-aged man who ran the place, the same who had grabbed me just now around the neck and dragged me away to deal with me in private as he saw fit.

What could I say? I was no thief, I was no cheat. Concealed walkie-talkie? No, sir, not me. Look, nothing in my hand, nothing up my sleeve... Come on, I was just a kid infatuated with gambling, a kid who loved the lights, the smells, the noises, the promise of gold. Criminal? If anything I was the opposite, an innocent delegate from the opposition on his annual outing, seeing the sights, paying my respects. Instead of roughing me up, as he seemed about to do at any moment (and I thought of that deep, deep pond with the pedal-boats bobbing innocently on top), this red-faced gorilla should have been sitting me down to enquire after business, to swap stories, to trade trade secrets and tips...

This entire fantasy took maybe five seconds to voice itself in my head—during which I realised I'd breathed my last breath.

All of a sudden my sister Mary burst in.

How had she found me?

She grabbed me. "Mammy's looking everywhere for you. Mammy's going to kill you. You're for it now."

The gorilla was so shocked, as I was, and terrified now, and my sister so determined, that neither of us dared stand in her way. In seconds she had me out of there, swimming against the current of music and lights.

It would be a lie to say I did not look back: I'm sure I must have done. But we were moving so fast that all I saw—like all I remember now of what followed—was a blur. A man with one arm, the man beside him with three...

When a change in the law in the late 1970s brought one-armed bandits to every lounge bar and back room in the land, including Sullivan's down the street and half a dozen other places around the town, though I frequented them (like others of my age) it was only ever to play pool or talk to girls.

Is it Yourself?

—Howya?

—*Not three bad.*

—*How's she cuttin'?*

—Like a lawnmower.

—*Any scéal?*

—You know what I'm going to tell you? Divil the bit.

Sitting in the downstairs front room (always known to us as the Breakfast Room) with my eyes closed, I can hear them outside in the street, the light-traffic, spring-Saturday morning opera, the chorus of stop-and-nod and brief exchange, the great solos of laughter, the scandalous gossip, the hilarious carry-on of the night before. I try to hear the way they greet each other but over the sounds of even just occasional traffic it's hard to make them out.

Do they always, or even ever, address each other by name? Do they say, "Good morning, Mary," or "Begor, Tom, you're looking fresh and well today"? Or could everyone be like my father, gradually leaving names behind like so much unnecessary baggage?

For as long as I can recall living on Main Street, only a handful of adults ever call me by name—Mary Murray in Finnamore's fruit and veg shop, Mr and Mrs Dempsey next door to that, Sadie in Fortune's newsagents across the road... Beyond that immediate local circle, it is as if all of us Boran kids merge into one, as if there is no real point, or reward, for adults in trying to distinguish one of us from another.

Accepting his lot our butcher neighbour, for instance, only ever addresses any of us as "Young Boran there," both an acknowledgement that he knows who we are and an admission that it would be punishingly difficult if not downright impossible to learn all of the names of the hundred-plus kids that in these days still live along the street.

Among our near neighbours, the Bennett twins—or Pat, at least—exploits the system brilliantly, on the day of his First Confirmation doing the rounds, hand out, first as himself and then as his brother Willie.

Further up the way, the pretty Burns twins—think Pocahontas looking in the mirror—if they have developed similar tricks wisely keep them to themselves.

Our father too has his own system for negotiating the rapids he is likely to encounter upon merely opening the hall door. Twenty or thirty years before Alzheimer's sets in, he has devised a method for dealing with the problem of matching names to faces and faces to names. He deftly side-steps it.

"Well, if it isn't... yourself," he says, with a broad, winning smile, then proceeds with a compliment, "Begor, you're looking well," before turning the tables entirely, "And how are they all at home?"

And everyone knows *his* name, my father, Nicholas Boran, the man with the winning smile.

Sticks And Stones

In the corner house on one of the roads we passed on the way to primary school there lived (possibly on her own) an elderly woman who had the great misfortune not to ignore the taunts of passing schoolboys of my age but to give them chase instead. When precisely the woman had been singled out for teasing, or when it started to become something more than mere teasing, is anybody's guess. In the history of a town, a road, a street, who makes note of the day the doorbell first rings or the doorknocker sounds but no one is there?

Certainly the practice of stopping off before the corner house to make some kind of mischief was already well established by the time I transferred to the school and my new classmates and I found ourselves being trained in by the behaviour of the older boys in the classes ahead of ours. Just as in the schoolyard and bicycle sheds, so too were there protocols to be observed on the road to school itself.

Where in the beginning they had probably still teased and called her by her actual name (Annie T_____ or Nanny T_____, as I believe it was), a resemblance (in terms of age and stature, at least) to one of the characters of a new children's television programme quickly distinguished her from all the other similarly harassed but quickly forgotten old ladies across the town.

That children's television programme was *HR Pufnstuf.* Now rarely screened—even on digital cable channels with their endless, apparently random repeats—from September 1970 when it began its run on Irish television it achieved an almost instant cult status, certainly among kids of my age group (7 to 10 or so) in Portlaoise.

In the programme Witchipoo was the wicked tormenter of the hero, a boy named Jimmy who'd been marooned on an island over which she ruled with menacing laughter and a sinister hand.

By giving the name Witchipoo to the woman on the corner, some boy, perhaps from my own class, had allowed the rest of us Jimmys to see her as equally alien, equally unreal, a creature not governed by the laws or polite conventions of our world. It also granted a license to persecute her to anyone who would accept it. And with a whole school full of us just up the road—three hundred or so boys full of "vim and vigour", as Brother Creedon was fond of saying—sadly there was no shortage of volunteers.

Like a storm that begins drip by slow drip on a flat roof or against a windowpane, gradually the pressure on that one woman and that one small nondescript house built and built until, within a year or so, the dogs of St. John's Square and the Borris Road, of Dr. Murphy's and St. Brigid's Place were howling in sympathy with her pain.

Knocking the door and running away. Knocking the door and calling her names. Knocking the door, standing in the middle of the street and screaming her name. It's hard to credit that, through repetition alone, such simple irritations could inflict such torment. Eggs against the windows, eggs through the letterbox, plants uprooted, milk bottles knocked over, water bombs, flour bombs, graffiti scratched on the gate...

And through each and every one of these escalating attacks, the woman we had nicknamed Witchipoo—the woman we had branded Witchipoo—would come charging out of her house, predictable as a clockwork figure, waving her walking stick like a cudgel above her head to what, from a distance, must have sounded like the screams of adoring fans.

Even those of us who hated it—the drawn-out baiting, the whole cruel business—despite what other adults said, we were afraid of her as well and trapped in the margins of the game, the simple act of walking past her house enough to send her into a terrifying rage.

Where the television news at night showed Belfast or Derry, youths taunting British squaddies, waving sticks and throwing stones, daring them to strike, an aerial view of St. John's Square or the lower Borris Road from the same period might have revealed a strikingly similar pattern: the magnetic attraction of trouble, the helpless flailing or sudden striking out of those entrapped, the noose of school children gradually tightening.

Kilminchy: Wildflowers and Bats

1. Wildflowers

Rinuccini stayed there. Even people who knew little or nothing about Kilminchy seem to have heard that, at some time in the fact-stuffed cupboard of the past, one of the most glamorous-sounding names in Irish history had spent a few weeks in a big old house out the Dublin Road, nursing his wounds after the collapse of the Confederacy of Kilkenny.

Born in Rome in 1592, Giovanni Battista Rinuccini had not travelled to Ireland lightly. When he landed in Kerry in 1645, the Roman Roman Catholic Archbishop and Papal Nuncio brought with him two thousand muskets, four thousand swords and twenty thousand pounds of gunpowder—a massive arsenal by the standards of the time. Less clergyman than military organiser, his express mission was to direct the Irish Catholic Confederates—and elements of the Old English order—to rise up against Protestant rule, though the one conflict he had failed to prepare for was the in-fighting among the forces he had come to assist.

From the first time I heard of Rinuccini, in a first- or second-year history lesson, I imagined his arrival at Kilminchy under clouds of defeat, disgrace and bitterness. One historian tells us* that his departure from Kilkenny in May 1648 was "almost like an escape, as he climbed the town wall, which ran along at the back of his house, and, descending at a gate, went to Maryborough".

With the Confederacy in disarray, and the threat of even darker times to come, Rinuccini's anger that the Confederates'

90

Supreme Council had chosen to accept a ceasefire ("this unjust and pernicious cessation", as he termed it) led to the excommunication of everyone involved.

The historic event took place on Wednesday, May 27th 1648 at Kilminchy House. Within days Rinuccini had packed up and gone, his mission a failure, his days in Ireland numbered.

If he noticed them at all, no doubt he was little consoled by the profusion of bright May flowers that would have adorned the hawthorn hedges, or the primroses, dandelions and buttercups all around that between them aped the colours of the papal flag, yellow and white, spreading as they did in all directions as if to suggest that the entire landmass of Ireland had kept the faith.

2. Bats

Far enough out of town to feel remote, and set back from the road enough to make it seem mysterious in its vestments of blossom and shade, Kilminchy was a place I never really knew as a child. Despite the fact that my mother was a niece of the owner—and therefore must have been familiar with the place in her own youth—I can recall visiting it only once, an occasion almost guaranteed to leave an impression on a young mind.

It was a mild Monday in November 1970, still closer to autumn than winter. Dressed in our Sunday best (my brother Peter in his previous year's confirmation suit) we'd driven out the Dublin Road to the old house of my mother's uncle, Frank Gowing. That my father also had a brother named Frank meant that references to 'uncle Frank' in our house always caused me problems, and possibly added to the confusion that we were going to see someone who lived—didn't he?—in Michigan, four thousand miles away...

I remember my father parking the car, the group of us walking slowly up the drive among about a dozen others, similarly attired, to whom my parents nodded in recognition and spoke quietly.

Inside the house we followed in silence, climbing what I remember as a steep, low-ceiling'd staircase to emerge in a room in which, suddenly, we found ourselves face-to-face with the dead man, stretched out on his bed, old pennies holding his eyelids shut.

From the scar where his ear should have been we understood instantly which uncle Frank it was that had died. For if I knew only one thing else about my mother's uncle Frank, it was that he had only one ear, that the other had been knocked off by a stray golf ball (I'm sure it was he who had told us that) or by a bullet in the war (but which war?) or by an accident with farm machinery... The story changed depending on who we asked. I remembered him years before sitting in our kitchen, talking with my mother, drinking tea one afternoon, and my brother and myself sitting staring at his missing ear, or at where his missing ear should have been.

And now there we were again, staring at its absence, tempted to reach out and touch that knot-like scar, the candles flickering on the dresser and dancing in the patina of his polished shoes.

Tea and sandwiches, buns and cake. Strange women checking to see were we all right, filling our glasses with lemonade and orange crush. Men in small groups stood in the doorways, brushing late-season midges from their faces, laughing at low volumes, smoking in long, measured breaths.

Someone said there were bats overhead. On the driveway as we walked back to the car, my mother held her headscarf tight around her skull. My mother was afraid of bats, though she knew them well; there were bats in our own yard, in the outhouses and sheds, though my mother seldom visited them after dark. Even I knew bats, from a distance at least, seeing them in silhouette on those few evenings we'd return home late from some outing and had to run from the car down the long back yard through their swooping gauntlet of wings.

But my fear of bats was a play-fear, an excited fear. Even at that age I knew they did not attack people, did not tangle themselves up in your hair and have to be cut out, as my mother still seemed to believe.

Yet this was my first time to see a corpse, and in that unforgettable episode, long before I heard of vampires or Dracula, death and bats became somehow connected. Death and bats, bats and death; the silence of that bedroom where my younger brother and I had stood open-mouthed; the unearthly stutter of bat language on the run back down the avenue to the car...

And 'uncle' Frank of the missing ear? Dead in his bed there, then and since, following wherever his ear had preceded him; the ear itself, in my mind's eye—in my sleep that night—small and wizened, impossibly leathery, and black...

The Swimming Pool

I learned to swim when I was 38 years of age. I prefer to put it like that, I learned to swim *when*... rather than I didn't learn to swim *until*... It's the difference between an achievement and a near four-decade battle with one of the most common elements on earth.

In June 1971, the first-ever public swimming pool in Portlaoise had just opened. Though it heralded, if anyone thought about it, the end of skinny-dipping sessions at the Sandy Bottoms, the Cat Holes and similar locations within an afternoon's ride from town, the attractions of such wild places paled in comparison, and from the day the pool opened it was the only thing on our minds.

It was 82 ft by 30 ft, the local newspaper enthused, and on playing pitches and basketball courts throughout the town kids like myself paced it out, trying to get a sense of what lay ahead. Throughout that summer, the queues were continuous, the noise and excitement and smells extraordinary, even from outside which was as close as I managed to get. (At that time, no one in our family could swim, except my father, just about, and *he* was unlikely to brave chaos like that.)

And so the summer months went by, we set off on our usual two-week holiday, sitting on the windswept beach at Tramore, paddling in the intemperate sea, having long since given up, even at that early age, on learning to trust the water.

Returning to school that September, the few of us who hadn't yet paid it a visit had to sit through the endless tales of our classmates who seemed to have done nothing other than swim and sleep over the previous weeks. "Laois is the only country that doesn't even *touch* a county that touches the sea," we were reminded again and again by adults who couldn't swim, as if that were excuse enough for their not teaching us.

As it turned out, we didn't have to wait for long. A few days back into our old routine, the shorter evenings already closing in, one Monday we were instructed to bring in our 'togs': our next PE session would take place in the Swimming Pool.

Through good fortune (and perhaps town planning), the school and pool were almost in sight of one another—both of them built to facilitate the rapid expansion in that part of the town. So we walked there, downhill most of the way, at first in a neat file, as per our orders—out past the bicycle sheds, through the back gate, and down through St. Brigid's Place, down through, as it was known, Hungry Hill. The journey took no more than ten minutes, despite the occasional reprimands and threats from teachers that we would all have to turn back "if people don't hold hands", a journey filled with such expectation that the moment we spied the fabled building's grey-roofed, almost entirely windowless form, even the non-swimmers among us started to run and, had we been free to, we'd have charged through its swinging doors to leap fully clothed into its shimmering depths.

What happened, however, was somewhat more prosaic. Once inside the building, for many of us non-swimmers excitement quickly changed to anxiety. The smell was overpowering, the noise in those white-tiled changing rooms deafening, as experienced kids shouted and cheered and stripped to the togs they had put on first thing that morning, before jostling their way out past us to be first to the pool.

Four or five of us were in a kind of daze. Someone's sister had warned him about getting something called verrucas, and we looked suspiciously at the glistening tiles. Some kept their socks on while they changed, which itself seemed to make them even more unsteady on their feet and raised the tension of the group as a whole.

"Right, lads, everybody out now together," a teacher called. Rigid, white-faced, we made our way towards the pool.

Eighty-two by thirty feet had sounded big, and it was. But what struck me then, of course, and should have struck me before, was not the size of the pool of restless blue-green water, or the height of the sheet metal ceiling (besides the prison, and the church, surely the biggest indoor space in town). What struck me, and hard enough to take away my breath, was its depth, shallow at the point we'd just passed, but here before us, where the teachers had lined us up along the wave-lapped edge for a last-minute talk, unfathomably deep.

"Now, listen up," Mr Melia or Mr Booth was calling above the clamour of the echoes and reflections, though all of our voices were mixed together then and we were just a mixed-up herd of creatures at the edge of water, where any safety lecture that had to be delivered would have to be delivered fast.

Standing beside me in the line was my classmate Tommy Lawless, a handsome, good-humoured, sallow-skinned youth. The opposite of me—muscular, robust and athletic—he might have posed for a Renaissance statue and stood for eternity in the piazza of a sun-drenched Italian town. Given his enthusiasm for the task ahead, and his reputed prowess in the water, I felt somewhat reassured to be positioned at his side.

However, no sooner had I tip-toed carefully to the water's edge, to gaze down a moment, gazelle-like, into the ripples below (trying to estimate the distance from surface to tiled depths) than young Adonis himself, whom I had always liked and liked even afterwards, with the slightest of efforts, the most casual of gestures, tipped me off balance and into (and I see it again and still as if it was just now this morning) the glistening, blue-green depths of the pool, in a slow-motion spread-arm descent which, ironically, rather than drowning me, would strand me on dry land for the next thirty-one years.

Broken Biscuits

Apart from own doorway, the doorway of Lewis's pub just across the street was the one my father was most likely to pass through in any given day. But it was a threshold a couple of buildings further down that, six days a week (and often more than once a day), my mother, one of us children when we got older, or our nannie Ann Whelan would have to cross in search of the many things a large household like ours had need of from day to day.

In White's, a shop almost perfectly symmetrical with a counter on either side and display stands in the centre of the floor, one could find washing detergents and breakfast cereals (Corn Flakes *and* Rice Krispies), tins of black or brown or oxblood polish, boxes of matches, ham off the slicer, corned beef, loose tea, three or four fresh vegetables, blackjacks and jellies and, for my father, boiled sweets either by the packet or the pound.

Perhaps most remarkable, and sensible of all, in the centre of the floor in one of those imposing box-like displays with the hinged glass lids, the thing we loved to be sent across for most: shovelled up with a small tin scoop, straight from the factory or the factory floor, White's famous (to us, at least) assorted broken biscuits.

While the annoyingly memorable advertising jingle promised 'Kimberly, Mikado and Coconut Creams, someone you love would love some, mum', we were more drawn to the mixture of fragments that White's broken-biscuit box had to offer, and where surprise and chance and luck were everything.

Had we thought it through we might have prayed that the biscuit-making robots of the larger factories continued and even

97

increased in their levels of malfunction, creating ever more unacceptably cracked and chipped and otherwise damaged mounds of family favourites such as Bourbon Creams, Fig Rolls and the bristling-with-sugar Nice (pronounced niece) fingers.

The sole obstacle—and there is always an obstacle—standing between us and this chest of treasures was the man who manned the small wooden ship of White's Grocery for all those years, pacing its deck, hoisting and lowering its striped awning, sharpening its blades.

Tommy Ryan was a comedian who'd ended up in the retail business, a man who donned the white shop-coat of White's Grocery as if putting on a costume and greasepaint. Short, somewhat stout, a red-faced, bright-eyed, toupée'd man (though we knew not to look) he positively danced when you entered the shop and the bell above your head rang your arrival like the shot that announces some competition has just begun.

"Hello, Mr Ryan," we'd say, having practised the opening sentence or two in our heads while crossing the street. "Mammy wants to know would you—"

"Mammy wants to know?" he'd say, leaning on the rotary slicer, his fingers little sausages teasing its blade. "Is that right?"

And we'd answer nervously, "Mrs. Boran, Mr. Ryan—eh, Tommy…"

He'd flash us a hard-to-read look.

"Mr Ryan—" we'd correct ourselves immediately again, hopelessly confused now and worried we'd misunderstood the question.

And then he'd entirely change the subject, without warning, saying something like: "I have a lovely bit of fresh ham here, just in this morning. I'll give you half a dozen slices of that as well." And he'd take up the ham, the size of a skull, tossing it from one hand to the other to show it off, before slapping it down into the slicer and starting to cut so fast the noise of the spinning blade would drown out our protests.

Inevitably, five minutes after we'd gotten home with potatoes, maybe a small bag of broken biscuits, and now half a dozen slices of ham as well, our mother would be back to Tommy with the ham, and Tommy would dance visibly on seeing her come in as well, teaing and flirting with her, trying to tell her a dozen different yarns... so that it was hard to know if the small extra sale or the even smaller amount of attention was what he really craved.

Almost always she came home without the ham.

On one occasion, as my mother likes to remember, young Ann Whelan was sent over with the list and, as usual, immediately found herself startled by the blinding lights of Tommy's display. Though our housemaid or home-help (or whatever today's term might be), young Ann being only a girl herself was much less able to deal with Tommy than my mother was.

So when she arrived back, beaming, shopping bags in hand, and proceeded to produce every single item on the list—potatoes, sugar, carrots, Oxo cubes—it seemed that this time the victory had somehow been hers.

Until my mother noticed the bag of biscuits wasn't there.

"Oh," said Ann, oblivious to having taken a direct hit. "Tommy says he hadn't time to break them today."

The Slurry Pit

For most of my mother's adult life, Peggy Bennett was one of her dearest friends. A warm, talkative, good-humoured country woman, Peggy was often to be found in our house, agreeing to take a cup of tea so long as my mother was also having one too, and then only "in her hand" as she would be sure to insist. (The mental image delighted us children who imagined the pair of them like circus clowns, pouring hot liquids into each other's cupped hands.)

Such visits usually took place on Saturdays or when the tough farm routine afforded her some time and she came into town to do the grocery shopping. After she had completed the items on her list, her considerably more quiet-spoken husband Paddy, or their son Joe, would show up to collect her, usually declining my mother's offer of tea but often persuaded to sit down long enough to allow the two women to chat.

The subject, as might be expected, was usually neighbours, family members, some mutual friend or acquaintance from the distant past, for they'd know each other for the best part of fifty years. Sometimes Peggy would introduce a subject my mother was not entirely familiar with: land deals, for instance, or something to do with farm machinery. Then my mother would smile patiently and wait. For she knew, as friends do, to allow the story to conclude in its own time and that it might be followed by a story that would entertain her for a week.

The friendship between my mother and Peggy Bennett was undoubtedly cemented by the fact that, to the best of my knowledge, no fewer than three of my four siblings attended school for some period with one of the Bennett offspring. On those occasions, therefore, when we visited them on their farm at Coolnamona, there was never any shortage of things to talk about.

And no shortage either of things to eat. Peggy's mouth-watering cakes, jars of home-made jams and marmalades, bowls of freshly picked blackberries, a box of eggs with the feathers still clinging to the shells... We townies sat around spellbound and somewhat daunted by the fruits of her casual alchemy, excited and a little hesitant when her husband Paddy agreed it was time to show us the sights including, I thought I heard, a new young calf.

There was a new calf! Had I not been listening, all day, all week? There I was wearing slip-on shoes and everyone else now suddenly in Wellingtons, ready to head out!

"Be careful now of the silage pit," my mother said, so calmly that I had to look at her to see if she'd said it just now or at some time in the distant past.

Even townies like us had heard the horror stories, about kids—farmer's kids or townie visitors like myself—out playing for an afternoon in a farm yard only to slip and fall, stumble and vanish forever into a pit they hadn't even known was there in front of them... Suddenly the lack of wellingtons seemed like a very minor problem indeed.

But wasn't it all right? Couldn't I be careful? How dangerous could it be? And once outside, as I tip-toe'd along, wouldn't someone be sure to point out the silage pit? Dear God, let me not drown out there like a dog...

In the event everyone who left arrived back safe again. Having followed the two towering Bennett men, father and son, footstep-for-footstep across the yard, the small tour group of us passed through a red-primed low-hung gate that opened onto an outer yard and a milking shed in which the cattle were nowhere to be seen, as might have been expected given that it was the middle of the afternoon.

My father was talking about milk prices, quotas, machinery, reminding us that he too had grown up on a farm and knew his way around, or did back then before our entry into Europe had changed everything.

It started to rain. Saved by the bell, I thought, having seen enough. We turned back towards the house, the kitchen, the open range, a last slice of generously buttered fruit cake or rhubarb tart and cream the consolation for having seen no new-born calf, though I had, I was sure, at least discovered the site of the pit: not far from the house (as the horror stories always suggest), an area of strangely liquid consistency, and upon it a child's brightly coloured football, left there, I hoped, by a gentle country breeze.

The Zoo

The difference between town and country in a small place like Portlaoise was impossible to ignore, if only because the line, like the frontline of a battle zone, was constantly shifting and therefore under constant observation. Kids who cycled in from the country one week cycled home the next to the near edge of town, thanks to a terrace of new houses or a sprinkling of new bungalows which required the ongoing revision of our mental maps.

Outside of these troubling liminal zones, however, the differences between town lads and country lads were to us so patently obvious as to be almost beyond consideration. Town lads and country lads dressed differently, spoke differently, moved differently, as if their very skeletons and muscles were assembled and subsequently had developed in different ways. Town lads walked in straight lines, and their feet and legs and even the cheeks of their backsides had acclimatised to this movement; country lads on the other hand lolloped and swung, their distinctive gaits and long wide strides clearly the product of the open spaces to which they were heir.

Across the divide, town and country boys also had different ambitions and, in many cases, their very different futures were already mapped out for them on the basis of where they'd been born and raised: which parish, which townland, which end of a half-mile of lane.

Two small incidents, ten years or so apart—and both involving animals—might illustrate how some of these differences expressed themselves.

The Country Zoo is how I recall it, in the way that we sometimes label our memories in an effort to have return access to them. What it was really called I don't remember, but I do remember that one day in St. Paul's National School, up on the Borris Road (and therefore at the then edge of town), we were rounded up and led outside to the school gates not quite knowing what to expect, to find a small van, customised (to use a word that did not exist in its present meaning back then) so that instead of solid sides it presented to us a flank of hinged or fold-down panels behind which, in cages and cubicles of various sizes and proportions were about a dozen living creatures few of us townies had up to then ever seen up close. A hen, a rabbit, a small red fox... and creatures whose names many of us could not even guess (a badger, a pheasant, a weasel or stoat)... And while we stood there and stared open-mouthed, at first the country boys stared too, before quickly realising there was as much entertainment to be had in staring at us, as if we were in fact the exotic creatures there.

The second incident happened while I was still in the same school, but four or maybe five years afterwards. We were on what must have been the first of our few school tours, two classes of us loaded onto one of Johnny O'Brien's coaches ("No chewing gum. If I catch any one of you chewing gum..."), off to see the Curragh of Kildare—the endless grass, and furze, and grass and sheep, and furze and grass and sheep—then on to Bray to see the sea (a maiden voyage, no doubt, for some of us), and in which seaside town, overcome by excitement, first one boy then about twenty of us in all sent into a furious spin the postcard stand outside a seafront souvenir shop until the owner emerged brandishing a shillelagh and everybody ran, the promenade behind us strewn (I couldn't help thinking even as we ran) with hundreds of tiny photographs of itself.

It was the main stop, however, that provided us with the most memorable moment of the trip. For here, as the sign in the car park had it, were the legendary Zoological Gardens. 'The A-Zoo' as the

104

lads at the back of the bus kept saying, in what they imagined would pass for Dublin accents.

Monkeys and snakes were the early definite winners. Apart from brief infatuations with the sheer physical scale of giraffes and elephants (with their impressive volumes of steaming, straw-packaged dung) and, of course, the wow factor of the lions and tigers, the seals and polar bears, most of our time was spent around the monkey and reptile houses, in the former recognising least favourite teachers in the swinging simians and anus-stretching apes, in the latter simply delighting in the proximity of dozens of cold-blooded, slow-motion, lethal tubes of death, brightly coloured and dramatically marked, and on opposite ends of which we imagined we could hear (though the inch-thick glass) the tongue flickering between venom-tipped fangs and the distinctive rattle which was the last sound so many cowboys and Indians ever heard.

In these and other encounters, it was us against the world, boys against animals, no marked difference between town and country cousins.

Until it was time to leave. Having visited the gift shop, the pet shop and toilets, we were marched single file back into the bus, counted, counted a second time, told to behave ourselves and counted for a third time. Johnny O'Brien turned on the engine, the singing started almost immediately—'Old McDonald Had a Farm'—but just as the bus was about to pull out we became aware of a disturbance, an argument taking place at the door of the bus, between one of our teachers and a security guard from the zoo.

Everyone went quiet, not out of shock, or respect, but the better to hear. Just then a ripple of laughter went up from a seat down the back. We all turned around. The sound, or the lack of a sound—the engine being suddenly switched off—spelled deep trouble somewhere.

And as we sat there, backed up by our teachers the sullen security guard in cap and uniform came slowly down the aisle, placing one big hand on the headrest of each of the seats in turn, giving his progress through the bus the look of something vaguely ape-like in itself.

And even before he came to our classmate Pat 'Budgie' Keogh—an inveterate prankster, visibly trembling now with delight and fear—it was already clear that the game was up.

And before guard or teachers could utter a single word, extracting himself from his accomplices the bold Pat rose to his feet, at once class hero and class fool in the same tension-filled moment. And given that he lived then out the Ridge Road, where town and countryside met, one might say, producing from under his jumper a stolen pet shop bunny he was, before the country lads, the lunatic town, and a wild country lad to more sophisticated townies like myself.

Miracle on Main Street

Despite watching my fair share of it as a child, I think I've always preferred radio to television. The excitement of listening beneath the bedclothes to the foreign voices on my little Joy transistor far exceeded the dubious pleasures offered by our black and white set. For a start the thing itself was ugly, the picture 'snowed' all the time—no matter what the weather—and the fact that tissue paper would cling to the radioactive screen even ten minutes after it had been switched off was enough to convince me it wasn't all it was cracked up to be. On top of that I was already becoming short-sighted: radio let me do my travelling while my eyes took a much-needed rest.

This is not to say that there were not televisual highlights in my childhood. There were. Like the day my brother and I were brought to see the first colour television in Portlaoise.

As I remember it, it was a winter's evening and Michael and I—eight and nine years of age respectively—were upstairs doing our school homework and watching the old black and white Bush set out of the corner of one eye, when suddenly the door opened and in walked my father. We sat up in surprise. Only minutes before he'd gone across the street to Lewis's pub for his evening drink. It was most unusual to find him back so early.

"Now, me boyos, get your coats on," he said. "We're going across the road to have a look at something."

My mother appeared beside him smiling conspiratorially.

"A colour telly," she whispered, just outside of his hearing.

We were down the 11 steps of the stairs in seconds, struggling into our fur-hooded snorkel jackets like Scott and Amundsen, ready for the great outdoors.

Outside in the street the rain beat down. A policeman waved to my father from a damp doorway. We reached the pub. My father opened the door. We stepped inside.

The bar, usually a place of laughter and argument, was almost completely still. Behind the counter, the owner Phil Lewis and his son Michael, my own classmate, stood motionless. All around the room, men in caps and coats stared into space, pints going flat before them on the tables, cigarettes in the ashtrays dissolving into ash.

And then we saw it, over the counter, on a high shelf: the fabled colour television.

We stood transfixed.

There, on the screen, and only yards from our house, was a man and his dog in a field so green it was as if one might almost have smelled the grass. The man whistled between his fingers. The dog bounded forward, rounding up a small herd of sheep. *Green* sheep? Then the man came into focus, close up, and he was *green* as well.

My brother and I glanced at each other, then looked slowly around the pub at the admiring faces of my father's friends: Paddy Marsh, Tommy Ryan, Dinny 'Spokes' Kavanagh…. It was one of those moments where, even as a child, you knew the kindest thing was to say nothing at all, to let the illusion be.

Of course it wasn't really a colour television. In all likelihood it was an old black and white Bush set, not unlike our own. But, with a sheet of green acrylic set up in front of the screen, the longed-for miracle was possible.

Because they wanted to see colour, colour is what they saw, my father and his wise-cracking cronies, just across the street from where we lived back then, in a somewhat more innocent if never quite black and white world.

The Great Fire… of Maryborough

When Irish people remember the 1970s, nationwide strikes are among the first things to come to mind: postal disputes, railway blockades, stoppages by teachers, nurses, bus drivers, farmers and on and on… In fact, when almost 30,000 man-days were lost in the printing sector alone in 1976, there was a real possibility that it might not be possible to print sufficient posters and placards for all the other industrial disputes then going on.

Of course nationwide strikes were a feature of most European countries during the '70s, but Ireland being then, arguably, more an island than it is now, there was a sense that we were alone in our trials and tribulations, and this surely added to their intensity. Hardly a month went by without a national stoppage of one kind or another. And among the most feared were stoppages by Electricity Supply Board (ESB) workers who, unreasonably, felt the right to be paid a decent wage for what was, by times, a difficult and dangerous job.

As a youngster, living in a rambling, somewhat down-at-heel 11-room house in the middle of town, for me electricity strikes brought a kind of magical return to basics. Instead of the clean, flick-of-a-switch heat of a two-bar fire in a bedroom, or the instant illumination of a creepy bathroom, the sight of my father hauling in a gas canister or of my mother rooting in presses and drawers for misshapen candles was the first sign that the adventure was about to commence. The stately voice of newscaster Charles Mitchell would often be the last thing we heard before the radio and the house lights died in the same instant.

Now the challenge of surviving in the depths of the night lay ahead of us. And I loved it.

As one of the tallest members of my squad of altar boys, about that time I was regularly entrusted with the task of lighting the tallest of the altar candles and, on a couple of occasions, the Paschal candle itself (reaching up with a five-foot stick on the end of which was both a burning wick and a little metal hood to quench the flame). So there in the dark corridors of No. 74, naturally—or so I believed—the lighting of candles was a job for which I was eminently qualified.

As the moth to the flame, or Prometheus to the fires of Heaven, it was to candles more than any other household object that I was drawn, their little yellow dancing tears of light, their tamed flames hovering like, for all the world, angels on the heads of pins. My mother wound ring her hands wondering how she might cope with cooking for seven of us on a two-plate, turf-fuelled range. My father would head off on one of his endless expeditions in search of a working lamp. And I sat in the kitchen tingling with expectation, like my namesake St. Patrick adrift in the Irish Sea, looking forward to the moment when he might view the gift of light spreading out ahead of him from hilltop to hilltop.

The result was that, on at least those two separate occasions, I came within seconds of burning our house to the ground. Conflagrations were avoided, in both instances, by chance, through the good luck of someone walking through a door at the opportune moment. As my mother's thesis had it—as in so many things where wayward children were concerned—"The Lord was surely looking out for us".

On both occasions, aesthetics were part of my near undoing. For it was never enough for me to clear the bowl of a candle-stick (with a penknife, maybe, or the blunt end of a spoon), to hold a lit match to the base of the candle itself in order to make it drip waxen tears back into the bowl, and then—in those wonderful moments before the base could return to being hard and brittle and uncooperative—to drive the candle securely down into the bowl (causing the semi-molten wax to curl up or overflow into a tiny, rounded lip around the edge)... No, what *I* was looking for was some kind of accessory to set off my new trembling flame, some permanent and fixed object which might create a palimpsest of shadows moving in sympathy across the now radiant walls of our Neolithic home.

In pursuit of same, on one occasion I burnt a 3-inch diameter hole in the shade of a 1930s catalin standing lamp, a lamp that had stood for years on the mantelpiece in what we called the dining room, the noxious fumes bringing (I can smell them still) all the members of my family running in one direction, passing me as I ran, denying all involvement, in another.

On the second occasion, against my better judgement charmed by a kind of Victorian dream, I set down a lighted candle immediately beside the lace curtain of my mother's bedroom, further to animate the shapes and forms assembled there. This time it was the vigilance of my sister Mary that prevented my turning the house into a three-storey funeral pyre in which, though the others might have escaped, I should have gone to meet my maker, like so many of the old folks locally, wrapped in my shawl of Mountmellick's best.

And so it comes now as a considerabl surprise to discover in recent times that the greatest threat that old house ever faced, and survived, was not something of *my* doing during those power strikes but a fire of precisely one hundred years before and described in *The Irish Times* as "one of the greatest dangers that ever threatened the town of Maryborough".

It was on the night of August 2nd, 1878, about a quarter to nine, as it happens, that "an exceedingly threatening and dangerous fire broke out... on the premises of Mr. John T. Phelan, T.C." (he being the first husband of my great-grandmother, Anne T. who,

111

following his death, remarried, this time my great-grandfather John Delany from The Heath, Portlaoise.) Because the house occupied a central place on the street, and therefore in the town, "the danger to be apprehended was imminent and very great".

As with the Great Fire of London, the origin of the blaze was believed to be a rick of straw in the cow-house where perhaps one or other of the family, John T. or Anne T., accompanied by their small son Willie and infant Kitt, had been engaged in milking and toppled a lantern onto the almost perfect tinder.

In any case, the burning rick took on a life of its own. "This quickly communicated with ricks of hay adjoining," as the unnamed writer of the newspaper report so memorably put it, the dry turf housed in the same quarters adding to the intensity of the blaze.

"In a short time all were wrapped in fire, and so high did the flames arise in the now dark sky that they were seen for miles in the country, and numbers of people rushed into the town under the impression that a great portion of it was on fire."

Presently the town engine was on the scene, followed by the police (Royal Irish Constabulary). They set up the Barrack engine two doors away in the "thickly inhabited" Lyster's Lane, from which vantage point water could be "played over the wall upon the mass of fire".

Mr. Tobias Bannon, grandfather of local organist Fred, in assisting the police "particularly distinguished himself. When the fire was at its very height he jumped upon an outhouse next the flaming straw. The thatch was quickly torn from the roof, Mr. Bannon, in evident danger, smashing through the rafters and woodwork"—and depriving the fire of further fuel and additional purchase.

Given that the buildings on the other side of the yard included another thatched house in which were stored "a quantity of paraffin and other oils, casks of grease, resin, boxes of soap, and candles [ah, yes, candles!], all appertaining to the business of Mr Phelan, which was now seriously threatened with ignition", the sundry fire-fighters must have felt that they were dealing with the 19th century equivalent of a time-bomb. And given the numerous burning fuses of hay, a time bomb was almost exactly what it was.

Viewed as such, the perils presented by such an array of flammable materials leaves my own flame-juggling antics of a century later distinctly in the shade.

In the 1970s, quick thinking—and hands—prevented No. 74 from going up in smoke; in the 1870s, it was the hands of "hundreds" of neighbours who saved the day, the house, the street, and perhaps the entire centre of the town itself. The water to quench the fire had to be carried all the way up the street from the old Mill Pond, a distance of some three or four hundred yards at least. One imagines, with the number of people involved, a human chain extending up Main Street, the slopping buckets passed from hand to hand in the kind of co-operation that only the greatest dangers make possible.

And though by twelve o'clock the fire was "partially got under…" and the threat of its going any further stopped, the "matters originally attacked" (being the contents of the old sheds), like the guilty regrets of a schoolboy a century later, continued to smoulder through the night.

A Right Pair

The ownership of a large house in town (whatever its provenance, state of repair or the cost of its upkeep) brought with it responsibilities. My mother, who'd been in No. 74 since her teenage years, had embraced them from the outset. If it caused no obvious embarrassment to the women who called to our door requesting cast-off clothing, toys and other trinkets, why should it cause her any to do what she could to supply them?

Throughout the 1970s the two women who called to us most regularly on Main Street were known to every member of the family, and to most of the population of the town. Despite occasionally looking somewhat the worse for wear, even worn out by their endless door-to-door itineraries, the pair were always entertained at our house by whichever of us chanced to answer their call. Both were honest, genuine, passionate and if not employed or strictly employable then surely hard-grafting women, women with guts, and women who might suddenly reward the donation of a bag of old clothes or household scraps with a bunch of fresh flowers gathered en route to the house.

For years these visitations continued, never overlapping, the two women, possibly avoiding each other but seldom failing to show up on their weekly rounds, two separate bags almost always in our front hall or front room ready for collection.

On one particular occasion, however, the perhaps inevitable mix-up came to pass. Somehow my mother, in allocating the contents of the bags (based on what she knew of their respective family situations) had mistakenly included in each a single ladies shoe from a pair which no longer fit one of my sisters. Each woman duly took her bag, offered flowers, or blessings, then continued on her rounds before heading home.

Within twenty-four hours both were back looking for the missing, second shoe.

My mother quickly realised her mistake. What could she do? What could she say? She confessed it aloud, freely, openly. Both women, small-town rivals, dug in (as one might say) their heel. Moll had what rightly belonged to Nell: Nell had no business with what was the property of Moll. The argument went on for weeks with my mother in the middle and, in the end, all too predictably, neither gave in or took the first step on the road to a resolution.

Somewhere in the houses of each of them—who knows for how long—the two matching shoes, now separated, pined for each other. The two women kept them in constant view, constant reminders of what each of them lacked.

In due course, no doubt, they were thrown away—one to end up in landfill perhaps, the other on a fire… Unless of course, after the initial anger had died away, a third poor woman had called around to Moll's and afterwards called around to Nell's, her feet bare but goodness in her eyes, as my mother had seen in the eyes of both of them…

'Oft in the Stilly Night'

Growing up in a prison town, we were always aware of the presence, the threat, the attraction of the town's largest building. Though we were too young to grapple with the political situation that had given rise to it, as we headed off on summer evening escapades the prison was always there somewhere behind us, the dark, perhaps even invisible matter at the centre of our galaxy.

The tug-of-war between motion and stillness, between always going somewhere and simply staying put, while part of any youngster's life was, for us, amplified, made concrete as it were, by the castellated walls and look-out posts of a building that had been erected to restrain, to contain, to imprison.

In truth, I sometimes wonder if all sorts of apparently unconnected things might not derive their importance for me—at least in part—from their relationship to the prison.

There is, for example, the matter of my two favourite songs from my pre-teen years: the first about the joys and almost gravitational pull of movement, the second about its opposite.

'The Happy Wanderer' by British bandsman Frank Weir had been a hit in the 1950s, ten years or so before I was born. No doubt the fact that it was almost bursting with optimism endeared it to a generation of parents and teachers for whom the gloom of the post-War years was still a recent memory. Had they, or we, realised that the song derived from a German folk song—an unofficial anthem at one point for the Hitler Youth—it would hardly have diminished its appeal. For in the early 1970s nothing pleased us more than when our singing teacher Mary 'Nana' Claffey weekly lined us up, like so many scouts or soldiers— smaller boys to the front, long drinks of water like myself to the rear—and had us belt it out, staccato, for all we were worth, while Nana tested her ancient piano in the middle of the room with a similarly thorough musical workout.

I love to go a wandering along the mountain track,
And as I go I love to sing, my knapsack on my back.

This was in the Old Woodwork Room in CBS Tower Hill, a dusty, half-lit, panelled space, more like the hold of a 19th century transportation ship than the concert hall Nana seemed determined to transform it into. But even here, or especially here, that song uprooted us, lifted us, freed us from our individual selves and set us collectively in motion, the sprightly movement of Nana's hands on the ivories or beating time in the air, a rhythm a deaf child might have followed.

But there was another song, too, at the other end of the scale. Thomas Moore's 'Oft in the Stilly Night' was one of those songs that adults used to sing, and always wanted children to sing, but which children were rightly suspicious of. For one thing it was too slow, certainly too slow for three bench-loads of country lads and town lads struggling for balance while at the same time trying their best to topple the bench-load of singers in front or to the rear.

The second thing was that it was almost impossible to understand. Even if you somehow worked out what the individual words meant—'oft' meaning often; 'stilly' meaning still; 'slumber' meaning sleep— there was still that chain in the second line (like the prison hovering in the background?) or the bit where "fond memory brings the light", which always made me think of the usher in the cinema, shining her torch beam into our faces…

Yet every week, after throwing us the raw meat or the pure sugar that was 'The Happy Wanderer', Nana would move quickly on to that strange, puzzling song as if leading her classroom of happy wanderers into an enchanted, half-lit forest—to abandon them there.

And then one day, my preference for the first song over the second changed. It was April or May, I'm guessing, one of those bright, school day afternoons when you don't even bother to take off your uniform, just run in to the house, drink a glass of milk with a biscuit and hit the road again—off on some mysterious adventure or just off, out, away.

Whether that particular day's wanderings had taken me out on my bicycle to the Rock of Dunamase, or just on a circuit of the town, I don't remember, but suddenly it was almost dark, everyone was heading home, and as we wheeled our bikes up the slow incline of Main Street from the Bridge Street end, in the doorway of Hume's pub on the corner a man was singing. And, passing him, I was shocked to find I recognised the song.

For here again were slumber's chain, the eyes that shone now dimmed and gone, and the cheerful hearts now broken. But from the way he was singing—almost to himself, eyes shut, shoulder to the jamb—it was clear he'd been singing it for many years.

Though it was still late spring or early summer, here was a man singing of chains and darkness, of fallen leaves and wintry weather. Here was a man, stood in a doorway, half crying into his beer, yet somehow rescued by a melody that barely caused his lips to move or breast to swell.

Were prisoners ever released? Did they go home, come home, back to their lives? Did people recognise them? Did they still love them? I knew nothing of the answers then, and have learned little since.

In the last thirty years or so, I've heard Moore's song in a great many places: often in churches and concert halls, once at a funeral, maybe half a dozen times on the radio. But I often hear it in my head, coming home late at night, especially on all-too-rare overnight visits to Portlaoise.

And every time I see again that man in the pub doorway, prisoner or prison warder, or very likely neither of the above, but either way his happy wandering done, the laughter and bar sounds distant now behind him, above him the open sweep of a star-flecked sky.

Cloakroom

Even in a small town like Portlaoise it was clear that different families had different ways of approaching everything from diet to dress to housekeeping. Among the country lads for instance, who didn't get home for lunch, there was no one style or mode of operation: some brought with them barely enough food to feed a sparrow—a single ham or cheese sandwich cut in equilateral triangles—while others produced virtually whole loaves of bread, sawn in half and held apart by a wedge of butter and the meat of an entire small animal minus only its legs and skin.

And of both categories a good number traded, sold off or abandoned altogether whatever they had for the Golden Grill uptown and the luxury of a slow walk back down the street during which to dip their snouts in a bag of steaming chips and, standing on a corner, watch the convent girls go by.

Us townies of course took the hot food at lunch time for granted, arriving home to bangers and mash, oxtail soup or, early in the week, reheats of Sunday's casserole or, minced and now hardly recognisable, the left-over steak from Saturday's evening meal.

Then when Bradbury's cake shop crossed the street to trade directly opposite our house, we were all shocked to see the enormous numbers of country boys and girls who packed the place on schoolday lunch times and spent whatever pence they had on cream slices, chocolate éclairs and jam-filled rock buns, before heading back to school, still somehow hungry looking but, fuelled up on sugar, pushing and nudging each other now, sometimes scrapping on the road or in the playground, and often—when the sugar high had passed—going into a half coma back in the air-starved classroom.

Different families did things differently, I was starting to realise. Just doors away from us, for instance, the owners of a shop that sold fresh country produce which they grew themselves as far as we could see gave their kids almost nothing to eat, denying them even a single piece of fruit, charging the woman who worked in the shop for the single fresh egg she had for her lunch. And what made this meanness the more shocking was that in so many of the premises on Main Street we had only to walk in and smile to receive the offer or small free gift for helping our mother, some stick of liquorice or flat-head lollipop (which, to be absolutely clear, we always, initially, refused).

In the half dozen houses I knew well from visiting, it was clear that different families did things differently, from aiming all the armchairs and couches at the new television in one, to the whole room (almost the whole house) being focused on a crucifix or sacred heart lamp in another. In most houses just inside the door was a holy water font, though in many of them a curious finger was already more likely to return with a film of dust or cobwebs than a pearly drop of blessed Lourdes water.

When it came to holidays, the better-off families were already beginning to take occasional breaks in Spain and on their walls or mantelpieces might be castanets, earthenware jars garishly painted, tea towels that said Benidorm or Torremolinos, and in a press or underneath a bed where we slid in to hide we might find a giant brown suitcase, still with travel tags on it, the word Ireland at the end of the address transformed into Irlanda.

Beyond food and travel, and individual words and kinds of language permitted, forms of clothing were the other hard-to-ignore indication of family difference. Some kids, no matter what the weather, always wore short socks, or long socks, jumpers or T-shirts, canvas shoes in winter or heavy leather boots even on the hottest day.

One of the strangest things about primary school was the moment of arrival, first thing in the morning, when you headed straight for the quaintly named Cloakroom to hang your coat on its hook. From the moment you walked into that room, and smelled those often damp and therefore especially odorous coats, you could tell by just passing them, one by one, who exactly had arrived in before you, who exactly was sitting in his seat or down at the back of the classroom, looking for swaps of whatever was the latest schoolboy obsession.

This is not to say (or not simply to say, at least) that some boys smelled and others didn't, that some washed more or less or better than others. The differences that I could smell back then (and which others of my friends agreed were perceptible) had to do with far more subtle factors such as diet, household cleaners, smoking and non-smoking parents, modes of transport (car, vans and buses, for instance, compared to walking to school or coming in by bike)...

One did not want, even then, to make an issue of these easily navigated differences—not least because there were always boys, sometimes tougher or believing themselves tougher, who might wish to close down the discussion of topics that might not reflect positively on themselves. Even so it is true that such differences were noticed (if subliminally) by many, and one wonders at what point of our growth through adolescence into adulthood the awareness of such differences and distinctions began to fade away.

Whenever it happened, now and again there would be a small incident that brought them clearly into the light again. One such small incident for me was, for instance, a day when I accompanied my school friend Tony Conroy for the first time back to his family home on the Dublin Road, to play with his soldiers, flick through his books and records, and maybe kick a ball around with him in the grass out back, though he was always going to enjoy that more than I could hope or pretend to.

As it happened while we walked towards his house (slowly, no doubt, stopping to argue over the finer points of some schoolyard debate, or to stare up at the soldiers half hidden in their prison wall-top sentry posts), a fine fall of rain had gradually turned into a downpour, and suddenly we had no choice—having come so far—but to run now to reach our goal.

By the time we made it to the Conroy household, scrambling into the porch, ringing the doorbell, the two of us tumbling into the hall before his horrified mother, we were already comprehensively soaked through and through. Even the pages of our schoolbooks inside of our schoolbags were, I remember, virtually glued together.

But after that moment of common bondedness, of mutual experience, came a moment that set us apart and reminded me that, even in a town as small as Portlaoise, different families had different ways of doing things. Maybe it had to do with the Conroy household being modern, compact, well-built and well-heated while the Boran household was a rambling, breeze-whistling pile in which it was impossible to achieve true warmth. But when Mrs Conroy laid eyes on us in those first seconds, at the pools of water gathering at our feet, she immediately ordered us to strip to our underpants in order to dry our clothes before the kitchen stove or radiator.

And where Tony stripped to his Y-fronts, I remained fully dressed as I was (reluctantly parting with my heavy, sodden jumper). And though I told them, and myself, that it was OK, really OK, my repeated refusal of a dressing gown came as a surprise, even to me.

And later though I'd laugh about it back at our own house—how the first time I met Mrs Conroy I could hardly have stripped off before her just like that—the sense of just how hard it might be to step out of the prison of one's habits and one's differences was finally starting to make itself clear to me.

The First Traffic Lights in Town

Portlaoise was going—as my sister Mary's phrase of the time had it—all 'mod'. For in 1972, when I was ten and the sight of Mick Dunne driving cattle up Main Street past our front window was still a recent memory, Portlaoise was to get its first set of traffic lights.

The wondrous installation would take place at the far end of Bridge Street (itself an extension of Main Street), and would make it possible, I heard my father say, to get from our front door to the new church without any longer "taking your life in your hands".

Preparatory work for the new lights provoked a good deal of discussion in the town, particularly among the older people who had long complained of the danger, the pollution, the worsening congestion that by times threatened to bring the town to a halt. No doubt their excitement now was due to an end being finally in sight.

And yet, as we had seen so often, when it came to technology my father, like so many of his generation, was easily impressed. Electric razors, wind-up radios his brother brought back from the missions, sunglasses that went from almost-clear to, well, not-quite-dark-enough, all of these were sources of amazement at first, and a day or two later things never to be spoken of again.

But even while we children stood slack-jawed in front of some of the gadgets he produced or which we found illustrated for sale in the back pages of *Astounding* comic books, we could not always be depended on to admire the things the older folks admired. When it came to what the magicians call 'the reveal', at times it was as much as we could do not to simply stand and stare and point and laugh out loud.

In the case of the town's first traffic lights, despite myself something almost mystical occurred when I first set eyes on them. We were on our way to evening mass, with no idea that they'd been finally wired up and turned on earlier in the day. Coming into Bridge Street—my father perhaps still contemplating the window display of the rival travel agency (little Dunne, as he called him) a few doors back on Lower Main Street—it was I who first noticed them ahead, hovering above the street, no, not hovering but on a silver-grey pole the colour of an apple tree...

And before I could say what it was that I could see, like Yeats' apples in the famous poem they were changing colour before us miraculously, green to amber to red to green again, the golden delicious apples of the sun.

Piano Lessons

The feeling, shared by a great many people, that music is a form of travel and might whisk one away to the far end of the globe or back a hundred years in time, is exemplified for those of us who had an all-too-brief encounter with a piano.

For if ever there was an instrument designed to suggest travel, the piano is it: that array of sprung pedals; that dashboard of monochrome keys like some futuristic cockpit; and, of course, the almost compulsory stool or low seat which greatly adds to the sense of a journey about to begin.

If tedious renditions of 'Ten Little Ducks' can be counted as singing, in the early 1970s I had long since shown signs of a talent for holding a tune (though turning one off was something else). Having in addition the optimum number of sufficiently flexible digits on either hand, I was duly enrolled by my mother for a course of piano lessons to take place in our upstairs sitting room where an upright instrument of recent purchase provided a platform for vases of flowers and a place to keep First Holy Communion photographs out of our reach.

Ena Moore was the piano teacher, a thin, always scarf-and-coated woman who travelled everywhere by bicycle, in the basket of which would be a pump, a bulging satchel of sheet music and—in season—a plastic see-through raincoat, for all the world like one of those covers people seemed reluctant to remove from new furniture. Somewhat otherwordly—from my adolescent viewpoint at least—Miss Moore, as she was also referred to, and addressed, confirmed her aura of strangeness by determining to teach me, almost from our first encounter, not something by The Beatles or even something vaguely jaunty from a popular musical of the time, but the negro spiritual 'Let My People Go'.

No doubt Miss Moore was trying to raise my horizons, but I entirely failed to see how I might have been expected to respond to a minor chord dirge concerning, as even I could see, the enslavement of the Jews by the Egyptians, at least two thousand years before. Was I meant to read the song as a metaphor for the enslavement of children like myself, press-ganged into piano lessons one mournful note at a time when even the back of a thumb across the piano keys could produce a far more satisfactory, and voluminous, sound.

> When Israel was in Egypt's land,
> Let my people go.
> Oppressed so hard they could not stand,
> Let my people go.

Once again, the decades having passed, I find myself wondering if there might have been some significance in the choice of song, some relationship between the enslavement it recalled and the imprisonment at the heart of our own town. Were other children of my age in other houses around the country similarly doing time pounding out such sorrowful tunes, like so many negro prisoners on a Georgia chain gang? Surely it was more likely that the closest they came to bondage was Rolf Harris's 'Tie Me Kangaroo Down, Sport' or, a couple of years later, the massively popular and cloying 'Tie a Yellow Ribbon Round the Old Oak Tree'—a song inspired by the true-life experience of a homecoming prisoner in the States.

Paul Robeson, that huge-voiced champion of the Negro spiritual, whose stirring version of 'Go Down Moses' is known throughout the world, was himself the son of a former slave, not in Egypt but in 'the land of the free and the home of the brave'. His outspoken criticism of racism, his support for the International

Brigades in the Spanish Civil War, and his activism against colonial presences in Africa saw him branded a traitor and finished his career in the United States. Denied a passport in 1950, he had to say goodbye to his international career too, despite defiant gestures such as the time in 1952 when he sang a concert on the back of a flat-bed truck at the International Peace Monument outside Blaine, Washington, an audience of 20,000 gathered to hear him just yards away across the border on Canadian soil.

How much Miss Moore might have known about him, I cannot say. But it seems likely she would have been aware of even part of his fascinating story and the political implications of his repertoire, of which 'Go Down Moses' was only one small part.

Though its funereal progress was, certainly back then, too much (or too little) for a boy like me, I remember there was a small tremor of excitement when it came to tracing out the melody: against the background of an E minor chord, moving from E up to C, back to B and up to C again before coming to rest on the A, white keys all; and then, instead of repeating the pattern, after the signature, and on the way to A for a second time, the unexpected rise to G sharp, the first black key in any tune I'd tried to learn.

It would be too much to say that this transition held any special power over me then, or indeed had any political intent—though it's hard to listen to Robeson voice the word 'people' at this point in his recording of the song and not feel that it was for him a political departure. One might even imagine that he knew he was taking his listeners with him on a journey beyond the all-white-key landscape with which they were familiar—beyond the flat lands and meadows where Old McDonald tended his animals under the innocent reassurance of 'Twinkle, Twinkle, Little Star'.

And thanks to Miss Moore, Ena Moore, and that one then-unloved tune, I look back on those few brief piano lessons now less as a personal incarceration and more as an invitation to travel (an invitation that is still open)—fingers curved, wrists straight, feet planted firmly on the pedals—to places and times which, had they been explained to me in words, could scarcely have had such a powerful effect on my young if easily distracted imagination.

The Green Mill

Along with all of the sheds in the yard behind our house, my father owned a mill, complete with four-acre field, running stream, enormous iron wheel and mechanical works which, though still in place when he took it over, were long since rusted up through lack of use. Given that he had bought it to use as a storeroom for his expanding joinery agency, its provenance and present condition were more matters of curiosity than of any practical concern.

In a sense the Green Mill was a big old building without a past. We knew, or half-knew, that it had once belonged to Odlums, the famous milling family that operated the modern plant in the town (and where my mother had been employed before she married). Yet we were vague about anything before March 1972 when my father had purchased it from the Seymour estate (whoever Seymour was) for, as the papers record, the sum of £800.

And yet the Green Mill was an impressive building. I couldn't begin to guess how many thousands of square feet it covered—but it was four storeys tall, the precursor of a multi-storey car park, like four football pitches stacked one above the other, I often thought, and everything under a permanent layer of dust and pigeon shit. It also boasted a much-admired archway, just wide enough to facilitate an ass and cart if not every motorcar whose driver thought they might sneak through. From a distance like a prison itself, inside the mill was darkness, bats and echoes, wrapped in cut-stone walls as thick as a man's outstretched arm.

Even during the hours of daylight it was night inside. Above the main door you reached up to your right and drew down on a rusty, squeaky lever that controlled the 3-phase power to the place. The lights came on. Single bulbs dangled from cheap telephone wire, the grey and white wound around each other. And whether it was some problem with the power, or with that wire, each bare bulb used to came on in turn, with a slight delay, as if even the electricity was cautious about entering.

Being just nine when my father bought it, I was not yet old enough to help in the dangerous work of hauling window- and door-frames up and down three flights of stairs or of hoisting them on single-wheel pulleys to second- or third-floor openings overhead. My time would come, and sooner than I expected. But for the moment, despite being a building from the industrial revolution and in which my father himself seemed scarcely more than a slave, the mill was a perfect if slightly spooky place to play.

Eerie enough in the daytime, twice as eerie at night, on a stormy night the mill beccould beame positively terrifying. Sudden chills, strange noises, high-pitched whistlings through the very floors. The bats would get restless, the lights would flicker, and the trickle of water underneath the wheel would swell and flood, drain off and swell again. There were rumours of a horseman, headless of course, on the worst of those nights. Old Pee Lalor, from the nearest house, had seen it himself, a galloping figure coming too fast through the low, narrow archway… We closed our eyes to the image in our minds. He left it at that.

On many occasions we had come across or heard about cars stuck halfway in and halfway out, including a squad car in pursuit of thieves who'd robbed Alo Donegan's electrical shop up town. In daylight it was clear that only the very best of riders, like drivers— proceeding as if with nitro-glycerine in hand—might safely pass through.

Whatever about the general feel of the place, the story of the headless horseman (or horsewoman) didn't, for some reason, frighten me especially. Perhaps my time in the mill had already toughened me up. But it never failed to come into my mind when I found myself in the vicinity of that archway after dark.

And does it mean anything now to learn that the owner of the mill in the early 1800s, Sir John Tidd or Tydd, was also the owner of Lamberton House maybe five miles away at Dysart, wherein for many years a certain White Lady was to be seen carrying her severed head under her arm?

Time passed. We grew to the task. At twelve or thirteen years of age now, old enough to struggle alongside my father—to feel his displeasure, his anger, his occasional praise—emerging from a day's work in the mill we would invariably find darkness had fallen outside.

And in that strange post-twilight space I would wait for that rider, standing my ground and looking back to see the ghostly figure coming up behind us, at full canter, horse-drawn to his decapitation. With the sound of hooves already thundering off into the distance, looking up I would imagine the slow motion arc of his severed skull, the open mouth, the startled or horrified final expression, before feeling the soft thud as it landed at my feet in the carpet of yellowing leaves and burst-open horse chestnuts—like the eyes of so many ghosts staring right through us.

'View from My Window'

My brother Peter was something of a Renaissance man. The fact that he had yet to reach his teens did not detract in any way from the power he had over, and the awe he inspired from, my younger brother and myself. Where other older brothers went out in the afternoon to kick football with friends or somehow to vanish utterly in the finite spaces of the town, Peter would as likely retreat into a quiet room and within an hour be calling us up to see his latest discovery or invention: flash lights made by nailing an assortment of paperclips, wires, clothes pegs and bulbs onto off-cuts of wood; blueprints—à la Leonardo da Vinci—for machines to get him dressed in the morning (which started by tilting him gently out of the bed); and, in the years that would follow, mixing components sourced from mail order companies with household rubbish, everything from radio transmitters through crude synthesizers to a device made from old Corn Flakes packets (following a patent taken out in Prague in 1952) that harnessed pyramid power and the earth's magnetic field in order to keep razor blades sharp forever.

The line between art and science which the men of the original Renaissance had so successfully blurred was equally ignored by my brother, and if rain stopped him heading up our back yard to bury 3-volt batteries in the earth or to dowse for water with the aid of two sawn-off coat-hangers he was likely to be found in the front room, instead using the one always uncluttered table in the house for his easel.

And it was in that front room (the Breakfast Room of another time) that during the early 1970s my brother began to sketch for a time most days, recruiting my younger brother or myself to pose for him in portraits that, surviving still, reveal his raw untutored talent and our unconcealed delight to be the focus of his attention.

A variety of subjects attracted him, this art-struck adolescent, machines and automobiles prominent among them. There are line-drawings of our Roscrea aunt's Morris Minor 1000 (IFI 728), of the Gaze & Jessop delivery lorry (DCI 924), and, of course, of the first of our father's Volkswagen vans, the latter in profile and sadly incomplete, the outlines of the wheels lightly sketched in pencil but never firmly retraced so that, fittingly perhaps, the chassis seems to float there on the page like one of the half-glimpsed chariots of the gods.

For all of this 'on location' work, however, it is a drawing he made in that same Breakfast Room in 1970 or '71 that has the power to recreate that time and place, despite the fact that it has long since vanished. A prize-winner in the Children's Art competition that took place in the town every year—the exhibition of winners in St. Fintan's 'Mental' Hospital drawing hundreds of visitors over the course of the viewing weekend—'View from My Window' depicted the opposite side of Main Street as seen from the window of my brother's make-shift studio.

Drawn on a sheet from a large-format art pad (as opposed to on wrapping paper or whatever else might be to hand), the monochrome 'View from My Window' presented such a realistic view of the street that at first it drew *ums* and *ahas* of appreciation for its draughtsmanship and then, shortly thereafter, a respectful silence for its apparent belief in the value of the everyday. It is not too much to claim that 'View from My Window' earned my eleven-year-old brother the admiration of everyone who saw it: teachers, school friends, the town's population at large.

When I went with my parents to view the exhibition (where pictures were exhibited taped to the floor as well as hung on the walls—an indication of the phenomenal interest and number of entries), people approached my mother to enquire about the picture and to ask her to pass on their best wishes to the artist. The four or five business premises included in the picture themselves attracted considerable discussion. One could almost see the various denizens of Lewis's public house or Power's betting shop, who stopped to examine it more closely, imagining themselves on its smaller scale, reading the meticulously-reproduced notices in their windows or greeting each other with their customary *howayas* in those graphite-shaded doorways.

Of the street itself, people marvelled at the slight but distinct bowing of the electricity lines between poles, the familiar pattern of the paving, the expert framing of it all by the frame provided by the Breakfast Room window: here was a world that invited you in, even as it reminded you that you were locked out, behind glass, across the street, looking out through a window whose origins were in another century, another time.

What is remarkable about 'View from My Window' is that, along with the picture, and the house that provided the view, even the view itself is long since altered beyond recognition. Lewis's monochrome-fronted pub, with its step-around corner doorway and double swinging doors (saloon style) has been replaced by a building that looks more like a ferry boat run aground.

After decades which saw them on both sides of the street, Bradbury's cake shop has also vanished, taking those medic-like shop assistants in their long white coats—who must have trained for years to so delicately bag chocolate éclairs, apple squares and custard slices with a single pleasing shake and spin and tug.

There are, consequently, fewer bees and wasps on Main Street nowadays, though the hive of activity around Paddy Power's for the Grand National has only moved (as the cake shop had done) from one side of the street to the other. And the beehive haircut never did feature much among the sober hairstyles offered by the reclusive Miss Cussen, long since absent from her perch at her window from which she watched the future's slow advance into the town.

The ancient cloths and clothing, polished floors and brass-lipped counters of Burke's drapery would no longer suit, or fit perhaps, in our quick-fit world. Yet the ghosts of Peggy Meehan and her courteous staff remain there today, the baskets and pulleys of the overhead cash system conveying change from so far back in that cavernous store that, despite such advances in technology— despite science and art—they might well be obsolete by the time they arrived.

2.

Sunday 2nd December 1973 was a viciously cold day of what was already shaping up to be a particularly harsh winter. After November snow falls that, for the first time in years, meant we had actually built our first close-to-life-size snowman in the top yard (complete with carrot-nose, hat, scarf and walking stick), the snow had lately started to melt a little but then suddenly refroze so that much of the countryside, and the very footpaths of the town, by early December were treacherous underfoot.

Of course we school kids loved it, skating off in the direction of the Borris Road down the gradual incline of Main Street, dodging snow- and ice-balls thrown from the shadows of Lyster or Pepper's lanes.

But for those who knew Portlaoise only as the non-descript midland town to which they would come by coach and mini bus a dozen Sundays a year to voice their demands for political status, increased visiting hours or other benefits for their incarcerated family members, friends and allies, the freezing weather was just another sign of the hostile welcome that awaited them.

The tensions that had developed between protesters and Garda in similar gatherings over the previous twelve months suggested that the demonstration planned for 3 pm that afternoon was unlikely to pass off without trouble. And when some 600 provisional Sinn Féin supporters took to the streets, almost immediate scuffles between them and the estimated 200 Garda on duty in riot helmets and visors, first led to projectile-throwing during speeches in the Market Square and then to more determined widespread public disobedience. Windows were broken, missiles thrown at shop fronts. Newspapers reported an elderly couple being set upon by the mob (Portlaoise people did not want to give in to what was happening to their town). And by the time the protesters had made it to the other end of the town, a Garda car had been overturned and set on fire outside the house of our school friends' John and Noel Brown at the beginning of the Dublin Road, just a couple of hundred yards short of the prison.

"That particular day," John remembers thirty-six years later, "we were sitting on the wall, just up from the house, beside [his uncle] Bobby's. And we were looking at it all, and it was like a game... the marching and shouting and roaring, boys up on the roof taking the tiles off and smashing the windows, throwing them down..."

And when the protesters' route was blocked, and they tried to get through the church grounds, if anything the increased danger only provided further excitement for the children.

"I remember thinking that's great because, when they did the baton charge, they hadn't far to go."

John Brown was eight in 1973 and, like most eight-year-olds, living on a different planet than the adults who fretted and worried about such things.

"It was like a video game," he says. "It wouldn't affect you at all... You were forever hearing explosions in the morning... And every time the soldiers went past we used to call at them, 'Go on Dad's Army!' That was the way it was."

When Garda patrol car 1649-ZC was overturned and set on fire, maybe the Browns and other children were cleared away by adults suddenly realising just how dangerous things had become, just as the adults up on Main Street who at first persisted with their

Sunday stroll through town suddenly felt it wiser to take to their heels. Further windows were smashed, a second car was burned out outside Kennedy's the chemists on Main Street; Garda riot teams stormed a pub in the Market Square and dragged the occupants—protesters as well as locals having their Sunday jar—into the street.

From our mid-way vantage point on Main Street (from the very same lace-curtained, thick-walled, old world room where my brother had painstakingly created his monochrome masterpiece), with the smell of smoke in the street, the clamour of voices and sirens, of bottles breaking, and of literally hundreds of stampeding feet running back and forth, this way and that, all of it ringing in our ears—as we stood there and watched, horrified, a riot squad Garda's down-swung baton opened a gash in the head of a cowering stranger, like a spoon opening a hard-boiled egg, the unspeakable, indescribable stain spray-painting the glass—until one of our parents washed it off later that day, as if to reinstate, against the odds, the view from our window.

Tonsils

As a youngster, and particularly after watching one of my father's beloved cowboy films, like most youngsters I dreamt of going down in a hail of bullets or stumbling through the desert to the nearest water-hole, and help, a broken arrow protruding from my calf.

Some kids in school talked about killer clowns and surgical knives, presumably based on whatever films they had been fortunate—or unfortunate—enough to see when their parents' attention had been temporarily elsewhere.

But when it came to a first close encounter with mortality, never for a moment did I suspect it would come in the guise of a creature as cloyingly innocent, as utterly uncool, as Kermit the Frog.

My tonsils were the problem, my tonsils had to go. That was what everyone said, my mother and father certainly, but also the majority of their friends who in the course of a typical week would drop in for a cup of tea and a chat to find me in the kitchen yet again, laid out on the settle bed my uncle Tom had made, an item of furniture which though it turned the place into a hospital ward at least saved my mother a dozen extra trips up two flights of stairs in her endless shift as cook and cleaner, now nurse and children's entertainer.

"Oh you're right, Nancy," they'd say, tapping a wholegrain biscuit on the side of a saucer to avoid spreading crumbs. "It's the only course of action when it gets that bad." A sympathetic nod in my direction. "The tonsils will have to go, they'll have to go."

It was as if they believed that, by repeating it a sufficient number of times, my tonsils might pack up and leave of their own accord. Some nights I almost felt pity for them, my tonsils, red-faced bags of venom that they were.

It was hard, I suppose, to think of my tonsils as anything other than part of myself. For as many years as I could remember, I'd suffered so many sore throats, swollen glands, inflammations, white spots, red spots, tickles, coughs and fevers that, in many ways, my tonsils might be said to have defined me as the person I was. Certainly my miserably thin physique as a child, my lack of appetite and finicky diet to a great extent may be put down to them. Now they in turn were to be put down.

The prospect of having my tonsils removed was a strange one, not just because it frightened me but also because its repercussions were beyond my estimation. Soon, I told myself, the honey and salt and lemon, the mouthwashes, sprays, lozenges and pastilles would be things of the past: it was just hard to say what, if anything, would replace them.

Of course I took consolation from the fact that my sister had had her tonsils out some years previously and had survived the separation. But could I be sure that recovery would be the same for a boy as for a girl? How come I knew of no man—or no man living—who had been through what I was facing now?

"It's just like having a tooth out," my sister and others would reassure me, and then seeing my face turn pale, would quickly add further qualification. "It's not even as bad as a tooth because you're asleep the whole time."

Reassurances of this sort succeeded only in making me wonder how long a period this vaguely defined "whole time" might be. And once I let my mind start to drift at all in search of specifics, soon I would find myself in a dimly lit, spooky corridor at the end of which two bloated red dogs guarded the shadowy entrance to hell itself.

What prolonged the misery—and made it worse—was that every now and then, and at just the wrong time, I'd get better. The doctor would come, the consultation occur, the date would be set, then the swelling would mysteriously vanish. And once a doubt had creep in, the appointment would end up deferred and, finally, cancelled.

Even back then there was always some doubt about tonsils, as if, despite the operations they carried out almost routinely, even the doctors themselves were not entirely convinced that they served no real purpose.

And so, suddenly back to myself again, I would return to school for a week or two before, without warning, yet again finding myself back home, stretched out on the settle bed, my skin clammy, my head reeling, imagining faces in the soot stains on the wall, listening out for mention of the prison on the hourly radio news.

And this round of events might have gone on forever (the leavings, the homecomings, the rising to ruddy good health, the sudden reversals) except that in the first few weeks of 1973 some small germ caused a sufficiently nasty deterioration in the state of first one then the other tonsil (raw and virulent as solar flare-ups), that it was finally decided I should be put at the disposal of the County Surgeon, my bad-tempered lodgers to remove.

The hospital is about a quarter of a mile from Main Street, the one separated from the other by Ss. Peter and Paul's church, the prison and, opposite it, St. Fintan's Psychiatric Hospital, the other three major institutions in the town dedicated to overseeing one's path (direct or indirect, voluntary or involuntary) between cradle and grave.

We arrived in my father's equally ailing Ford Consul, my mother taking me by the hand while, in the other, carrying my pyjamas, half a dozen comics, and a face cloth, toothbrush and towel in what we called my altar-boy suitcase. The fact that no change of clothes had been packed was my first indication that this might well be an excursion with no return.

The hospital I recognised as the larger of the two buildings before us, the smaller one being the Midland Health Board dental clinic, a place that sent shivers down my spine and from which, having received his anaesthetic, my terrified older brother had once been sent home because the dentist on duty had decided to treat himself to an early lunch.

On the way in the main door, my father leading, we passed a man in dramatically stained overalls, rubbing a greasy slick off the side of his face with a handkerchief. He seemed to stare at me as we passed. The surgeon McCormack! I knew it the moment I laid eyes on him, but what terrible misfortune in the operating theatre could have left him in such a state? And if this was what the surgeon looked like... I wanted to run but, like a condemned man, my feet carried me straight ahead. (Would it have helped if I had recognised the man with the handkerchief and monkey wrench as Joe Conroy, hospital boiler man for a quarter of a century? In the mood I was in just then, probably not.)

On the ward I was escorted to were three beds and a cot, two of the beds occupied by elderly men, both sleeping, the cot by a bug-eyed boy about half my size who made up in volume what he lacked in stature.

"I'm the king of the castle, get down, you dirty rassal!" he barked at me the moment I entered the room, a line which, despite its lack of clarity (was it 'vassal' he was trying to say or 'rascal'?) he would repeat at regular intervals over the course of my stay, oblivious to the fact that, from my full-sized bed by the window, I had shown not the slightest interest in joining him in the confines of his cot.

With my parents gone in search of a cup of tea, or forms to complete, despite the reassurances of everyone I encountered I was not long in retrieving from the back of my mind the warnings of schoolyard friends and bullies whose voices whispered to me now threats general and specific but sufficient in number to set my mind aswirl and have my eyes espying glinting blades and congealing shadows behind every innocently fluttering nylon curtain.

To say I was frightened does not do the feeling justice: the only thing that prevented my climbing out of the window to join the circus or the foreign legion (both in my mind at the time as good career options) was my severe lack of energy (had I been doped already?), a trait which would surely get me to the show on time.

Of the run-up to the operation itself, I am surprised to say I remember little: being asked to sit up, being lifted onto a trolley, being spoken to by a soft-voiced nurse as I strained to wave goodbye to my mother (did I dream that last bit?). I remember going through the double doors of the theatre feet-first, receiving an injection and trying to count backwards from 10 to 0 but not making it even half way.

When I asked at some point what would happen to the tonsils, I'm told surgeon McCormack whispered to me that he'd give them to the hospital cat, which piece of meaty info I would afterwards share with anyone who would listen.

And of Kermit the Frog?

A couple of days after the operation, home again and in my own bed, recuperating with plenty of liquids and chicken soups, I thought to celebrate by getting up to watch Sesame Street on television.

As fate would have it, on that day's episode, four years after the popular programme first began, the glove puppet known as Kermit the Frog for the first time ever got up off his backside and showed his spindly frog's legs to his fans. And I laughed so much, as the saying has it, I though I would die.

Flypaper

Encouraged by the success of a jam-jar on the kitchen windowsill, into which a veritable plague of wasps and bees came to drown themselves each summer, in the early 1970s my mother succumbed to the dubious attractions of flypaper. Maybe it was the fact that, not long before, the Sullivan brothers had extended our small pokey kitchen, and the intervention into the structure of the house had resulted in the displacement of a number of hitherto unnoticed life-forms.

Mice, for example, dislodged from behind the old walls or under floors, were suddenly poking their noses into everybody's business; ants, whose nests had once faced out into our gravel-surfaced back yard, now re-routed their caravans across the kitchen table and up the kitchen wall ... Perhaps these were still the times before people lived in hermetically-sealed homes, buildings that sometimes appear designed to ensure survival in the void of outer space. Either way, the line between inside and out was still back then a fuzzy one, and flies were just one of the many fuzzy life forms regularly to cross that line.

The traditional solution to such incursions was a rolled-up copy of *The Nationalist and Leinster Times.* (This in no way reflects upon the literary or journalistic qualities of said publication; but as a weapon of broadsheet class it did offer a significantly longer reach—or greater penetration—into enemy territory than did the tabloid *Leinster Express.)* Where the whoosh and slap of paper cudgels, the cheers or curses of would-be assassins had punctuated previous summers, the arrival of flypaper had heralded a spooky silence in the house. Or at least that is what should have happened.

Where apples on strings meant Hallowe'en, and mistletoe signified Christmas, almost overnight the arrival of summertime was marked by a profusion of thin orange pendants that dangled from the ceiling as if the new kitchen were a cross between the Hanging Gardens of Babylon and the wondrous future the American comic books were still predicting.

First encountered in a paper tube, and tightly wound around itself, the new technology was primed by the insertion of a finger into a hole in its base. Tugged free of its own reluctance, it would suddenly drop through the trapdoor of itself to reveal a long, sticky single helix, the simplicity of which form belied its power to pronounce over life and death.

Ticker-tape our American cousins called the swirling, twirling, whirling lengths of coloured paper showered on victorious presidents and returned astronauts—though after one has seen flypaper close up, the implications of something glamorous in such motion become somewhat less convincing.

For flypaper, let's face it, was as ugly as sin. Where the generation of bug-zapping machines that would replace it at least attempted (with their red-hot filaments, their eerie blue screens) to dispose of the dead, flypaper seemed designed to show them off, making it the domestic equivalent of crucifixion.

And human nature being what it is, there was also undoubtedly a temptation to leave a hanging strip *in situ* as long as one could bear it, to see how many flies it was possible to accumulate, how many it might take to compose a living tongue of them, a temptation no doubt added to by the pressures of those earlier recessionary times.

And I remember too my older sister on one occasion at the dinner table standing up too quickly, momentarily failing to pay attention to the strip of orange doom that dangled above us all, the serpent eavesdropping on our conversation. Her screams as it first glanced against, then worked itself into, her hair, I can hear almost still, her screams as her struggling tore it from the ceiling and joined it more intimately to her. They were, it would turn out, a kind of keening for the death of flypaper.

For despite the *oohs* and *aahs*, the resolutions to get a pack for visiting relatives, the flypaper craze didn't last much beyond a handful of summers. And though my mother kept spares in the press for years, she never unfurled one again, and we survived the attentions of flies in the traditional way: swiping at empty air like mad men and mad women.

And at night, down on our knees in those years of the family rosary, we struggled to put out of our minds the images the television was bringing home to us now, bringing to us for life: the children of a land far distant, every one of them covered in flies, flies drinking from the wells of their eyes, and they without even the strength to shoo them away.

Bicycles Clips

1.

Bicycles all down the street, against every other shop front, two- or three-deep in places, the pedals of one poking through the spokes of another. And, where the thickness of the footpath paving permits, here and there the lone black silhouette of a messenger bike, nudged up on its stand so that it waits there all on its own— a faithful steed outside a Wild West saloon.

2.

Where the cowboys had their mustangs and bucking broncos, and the Indians their pintos, piebalds and skewbalds (great lovers of colour, the Indians), as kids growing up we had our parents' black 'high nellies', the occasional gaudily-painted racing bike or, after the visit of some rich uncle or death of some grand-aunt, a customized chopper, the latter a machine whose diminutive wheels placed one nearer to the road and therefore exaggerated the sensation of speed and mortal danger.

Admittedly less exciting than the thundering ponies we envisioned in our minds, a simple, solid bike had a number of considerable advantages. For one, it didn't eat or require more than very occasional maintenance, and for that maintenance the town had provided us with an unequalled champion.

Stories about unwelcome extra attention from one would-be repairman on the edge of town had long confirmed us in our devotion to Dinny 'Spokes' Kavanagh, and if anything needed doing it was to Dinny we would turn, a man who performed the daily miracle of almost blocking Railway Street with the vast quantity of banged-up bicycles he could produce from a workshop no bigger than the average box room. That Dinny's was also heated only by an open turf fire added to the sense of its being an alchemist's cave or smithy of old. And when Dinny grinned and nodded, talked out of the side of his mouth like a black-and-white movie gangster, it was clear that his wisdom went beyond words or language, and that his hands—like those of O'Dowd the shoemaker, or Jack Nolan a decade later, or Larry Fitzpatrick the mechanic—might prove themselves in utter darkness so well did they know their subject and its terrain.

That a bicycle left in for repair might not be ready when the young rider was keen to have it back perhaps goes without saying. But the wound of youthful disappointment is often healed by the light of the moon, and the following day a bent fork or slack-jawed brake could be good as new, and the wheat and the grasses and the trees in the fields would be waving us on to the chequered flag of a cheesecloth shirt knotted around a branch.

When it came to their advantages, bicycles were also considerably cheaper than horses. They could be stabled in the small yards and gardens typically available to town-dwellers. In pursuits they could be carried across plank bridges or hefted over low walls. And they had a greater chance of surviving the many shocking potholes on the back roads where we liked to play or train or battle (depending on who was there and what the mission was).

Bicycles could be fitted with accessories, too. Bells were understandably popular in a time when traffic was far lighter and quieter, car alarms and house alarms and ringing mobile telephones being still the stuff of science fiction. Some youngsters, myself included, who didn't have their own racing bike, tried putting racing handlebars on old upright frame, inevitably with disappointing results.

Those who fixated on the idea of optional extras could graduate to flags, pennants or rear-view mirrors: most made do with those little 1-inch coloured plastic tubes (cross sections of drinking straws worked just as well) that clipped on around the spokes and ran fluidly from hub to rim with a pleasing ticking sound as the wheel revolved.

And if one cycled fast enough, then those little tubes remained stuck firm, held in place by the centrifugal force of a spin down Lower Main Street, a sudden right onto Well Road, across James Fintan Lalor Avenue and out the Timahoe Road in the direction of the mart, (without once touching a foot to the ground, like Oisín and his friends on a flying visit to Tír na nÓg).

But, accessories aside, the best thing of all about bicycles was that it was possible to ride side-saddle, and for some distance, in a way that seldom really worked out with horses in cowboy films where women mostly, perched up there against their wills, could do little but cling on and hope when a slap on the rump from some unshaven thug sent their four-hoofed transports charging off towards the horizon and inevitable downfall.

For us, on the other hand, going side-saddle—feet stuck out in mid air parallel to the frame, or both feet stood on one pedal, whole body crouched down on one side of a 45 degree tilted bike as it raced downhill—was a kind of exhilarating initiation. And there were few better places for it than on the hill descent from the Rock of Dunamase.

Starting up in the loose gravel before the small Church of the Holy Trinity, you kicked off hard towards the sudden steep gradient where the road began, to feel yourself almost flown down the hill, below you this or that farmhouse, this or that group of Friesian cows, an old water pump to the left, stray chickens to the right, here and there the bicycle ceasing its shuddering and wavering only to rattle almost uncontrollably again as you followed the curve of the road through more and more cows, unimpressed in their black and white vests like maps of the world on which Dunamase, and not Portlaoise, was the only place for miles worth mentioning.

3.

By the late 1970s, shortly after my sisters Margaret and Mary had become experts at it, in turn I discovered the joys of youth hostelling, taking up membership of the Irish Youth Hostel Association, picking a hostel from the members' handbook (no photographs, descriptions alone) and heading off on a combination of buses, trains, hitching and shank's mare (as people used to say of going anyplace on foot), the great outdoors and, at the end of the day, an unheated dormitory beckoning.

Then, for whatever reason, one fine Bank Holiday weekend, sometime in 1978 or '79, a few of us decided to head off together, for Glendalough as it happened, but this time by bicycle, and bicycle alone, the plan being to cycle in convoy the entire way, a distance of close to 50 miles, despite the fact that none of us had ever really cycled anywhere before—except in circles around town, looking for distraction, cat-calling to each other, or practising 'hand-brake' turns in the gravel outside Coughlan's sandpit.

As luck would have it the weather was with us, most of the day at least, and it took us most of the day to get there. After the first few miles of tomfoolery, of singing the latest pop songs, repeating the latest versions of the same old jokes, we'd made it only as far as Ballybrittas (barely a good walk away). Our legs and backsides were sore, the gentle breeze from behind us was already a building wind in front, and far from wondering what had happened to our friend JW (who had failed to turn up earlier at the rendezvous point) we were now convinced we had drawn some

150

kind of curse on ourselves for having teased him, over months and years, for his greater than average weight.

The long march of Chairman Mao, the *tóraíocht* of Diarmuid and Gráinne, or the miserable wandering of Lear on the heath all pale in comparison to our endless, relentless fool adventure which at one point had Sean Bracken lying on the verge, bicycle across him, pretending to have been hit by a car in the vain hope that some kind motorist might stop and rescue us from our plight, from the worn-out records of complaint we had become.

Somehow, at last, dusk dripped out of the trees, pooling in shadows at our feet, and Monasterevin, Kildare and Newbridge behind us, even Naas a thing of the past, we arrived at Glendalough, our destination. Immediately on glimpsing it, like St. Kevin and countless others down the centuries, we felt relieved of our load, freed of our burden, celebrants who had completed the pilgrimage before them… At which point the door of the youth hostel opened and who should walk out but our school friend JW himself, looking fresh and relaxed before our withered forms and equally withering glances:

"Oh, you've made it," says he. And before we can ask: "My mother offered to give me a lift up."

4.

If bicycles were a passion for us youngsters (and would remain so well into our twenties), they were near fetish objects for many of our parents. My father had, as will be clear elsewhere in this book, a sequence of old bangers, crocks, jalopies and other four-wheel embarrassments, but it was to bicycles, I believe, that he was most attracted. From a bicycle it was that he first fell, in the "top" (Market) square in town in 1996 or 1997, in what would prove to be his first minor stroke, in his late 70s still preferring to cycle to the Post Office rather than to walk the short distance.

As with many men of his generation, that love of—even devotion to—the bicycle was expressed in a single object, or in truth a pair of objects: his bicycle clips. Visitors to our house in those days seemed to think they had pressed a lever somewhere and had been transported into the past when they saw my father take those shining clips from a hook above the kitchen range, smooth his grey or navy-blue pants against his shins, and then slide his beloved bicycle clips deftly into place, their almost but not-quiet completed circles and turned-out lips an end in themselves, the omega and omega, one might say, of his expeditionary preparations.

The Local Colours

A quarter century after the end of World War II, the conflict continued in the airspace of Portlaoise, Co. Laois (Queen's County as it had formerly been known), the majority of the action taking place above the bed of my younger brother Michael who, by the time he was a teenager, had seen more dogfights and planes shot down than all the decorated pilots of both sides combined.

In the bedroom we shared at the top of the house, my brother went to sleep under a circling Submarine Spitfire Mk1a or a Japanese Mitsubishi Zero—and nothing holding either of them in place but a taut black thread, a thumbtack or a strip of Sellotape.

This is not to say that my brother was a violent or in any way warlike lad. In fact he was, and remains to this day, among the most laid-back characters I have ever known. Where I might, for instance, approach a spring garden with spade and secateurs, saw and hosepipe in hand, my brother will venture forth with just a hammock in a plastic bag and an hour later be as settled in as Tarzan between two trees.

But where model planes and—on the ground—tanks and solider figures had but a passing attraction for me, for my brother the interest was, if not quite all-consuming, then remarkably long-lived.

No doubt some of my brother's interest in the war was due to a certain obsession with the same conflict in the pages of the various comic books we bought in Fortune's newsagents, comics whose main ingredients were the adventures of lonely spies, lost battalions and pinched-in squads of British troops abroad.

Warlord, *Victor* and *Battle (Picture Weekly)* offered everything the young Irish boy child could want to know—and a great deal besides—about the fears and loathings, the pride and prejudices of our nearest neighbours. From the suave British spy Lord Peter Finch to the can-do readiness of Bomber Braddock and Squadron Leader Kane ('Killer' to his friends), square-jawed and stiff-upper-lipped this ever reliable cast of characters delivered jingoistic dialogue that bordered on the racist—as if ink didn't flow in the veins of their enemies as well.

Images of scowling Germans shouting 'Donner und Blitzen!' 'Britisher Swinehund' and 'Dumbkopf'—before, two pages later, falling to their knees and begging for mercy (like the inferior creatures they so obviously were)—or of Japanese prison guards sharpening their bayonets or burying prisoners in termite mounds up to their necks, though we couldn't see it then were the lingering shadow of war propaganda still passing like a dark cloud over the land, though the war had been over thirty years already and Ireland, now awash with that poison, had been neutral throughout.

And maybe that is why we let those comic books go and, in time, the action-frozen soldiers, the ships and the tanks. Maybe we had as much as we could take of that particular claim on our imaginations.

But the last of those planes my brother was slow to take down, as if up there in Main Street airspace every pilot was ultimately alone; and picturing himself in that cockpit my brother could see down below him the wonderful sweep of a landscape patched like a quilt: woodland green here, bogland brown over there, and, reflected in the small few mirrors of lake water, not Queen's County but Laois jersey colours, cloud-white and sky-blue.

Nine Frozen Arses

In October 1966, when I'd been just three and happy to repeat anything I heard with no pretence to understanding, nine members of the National Farmers' Association, or NFA, had staged a sit-in protest at the Department of Agriculture in Dublin, demanding government guarantees for the prices of agricultural produce. By vowing to stay on the street "until hell freezes over" (which proved to be 20 days) they unwittingly provided the raw material for one of the longest-running gags to be enjoyed in our house during the 1960s and early '70s (if, in the circumstances, 'enjoyed' is the right word).

What precisely the farmers were protesting for was of course beyond me at the time—as were most things that did not involve warm milk and honey. But the repeated radio bulletins and endless shop-door discussions I heard and overheard did help some details to lodge in the mind. There were farmers. They were unhappy. They were sitting down outside. For a long time, a very long time. And it was cold.

Question: What does NFA stand for? Answer: Nine Frozen Arses.

It was Joe Bennett, the son of my mother's friend, who was credited with the line, he being somewhat older than the rest of us and adept at coming up with the kind of slightly edgy, slightly 'off' one-liners adults liked to laugh about for days but, when asked, couldn't explain to save their lives.

Nine Frozen Arses. My mother laughed at that until she cried, dried her eyes with a hankie and cried some more. It was the first time we heard her use a word like 'arses' (a word we knew was bad) without any badness attaching to it. And in a house where my father had produced the strap when someone said 'bum', it seemed extraordinary that 'arses' was allowed to go unchecked.

But go unchecked it did, they did, at least between my parents, so much did they enjoy young Joe's word-game—even if, like parents everywhere, they soon found themselves gritting their teeth and trying to look the other way as the smaller one of us dared to repeat it. "Nine Frozen Arses, Da; Nine Frozen Arses, Ma." I suppose they were hoping that the novelty would wear off before the next unannounced visit of a passing relative or parish priest.

When visitors did come to the house around that time, and maybe even for years afterwards (the seven Borans from Kalamazoo, Michigan, with their famous 17 pieces of luggage, the five Borans from Irishtown, Kilkenny, my mother's two sisters from Roscrea, or whoever happened to be passing through the town) I'd be making my headcount while the table was set, hoping to announce when the numbers added up: "Look, Ma, Look, Da, Nine Frozen—"

"Paddy, would you ever go down the stairs there and get me a tea cosy?" or "Why don't you give Margaret a hand with the bikkies and cake?"

My mother would be on my case quick, keen to avoid the need for embarrassing explanations.

The first-ever polar bear was born in Dublin Zoo at the end of 1967. One very cold if not quite frozen arse there, I would have thought. But despite trawling my mother's copy of the *Irish Independent* or my father's *Irish Press*, I saw disappointingly few other possible opportunities to speak the line.

In March 1968, sixty-one people died in an Aer Lingus plane crash, three more in another the following June. (Was Irish air travel really so dangerous back then?) In January 1969, the Deerpark Colliery, the last of the Castlecomer mines, shut down its water pumps for ever and ushered in the flood. None of these life-changing events invited the comment with which Joe Bennett had so selflessly provided us. "Listen to the news," was one of the choruses in our house in those days, but more and more what I was listening to meant less and less.

Would I have been aware, that August, of the introduction of British Troops into Derry? Of the thousands of refugees, frozen and miserable, that just eighteen months later would begin to pour across the border? Wasn't I more distracted—weren't we all distracted?—by the arrival of the seven-sided 50p piece, by Dana winning the Eurovision, by bombs under statues of Daniel O'Connell in Glasnevin and Wolfe Tone on St. Stephen's Green? Bombs under statues? What did it mean? Killing I thought I could understand, but wasting bombs on statues...

My father began to complain again about his troublesome leg, his 'Gough leg' as he always referred to it ("My Gough leg feels like it's going to explode!"), named for a famous equestrian statue the IRA a decade earlier had bombed in the Phoenix Park, managing to destroy just a single leg.

To see these events set out like this in chronological order comes as a shock, a reminder that we do not after all experience history sequentially, but in clusters of thinly-connected events spread out over days and months and years.

Bloody Sunday, January 30, 1972. Thirteen protestors shot dead in Derry. Three days later the British Embassy in Dublin burnt to the ground... Arguments everywhere, on the street, in school among the older lads, about the IRA, about bombs, about guns... Black armbands handed out by the Christian Brothers... Graffiti in the bicycle shed, whoever it was meant for: 'Fuck the Queen'... Two lads whose names I didn't know stuck into each other in the yard, "Fight, fight, fight!" a ring of us around them like something out of *Lord of the Flies*...

All of this in this one cluster.

And making up another: the great VG Spectacular with 4 Raleigh Chopper bikes to be won... a cache of butter, close to one hundredweight, and up to 200 years old, found by Bord na Mona workers in Clonad bog... a dead cat dumped outside the door of one of the local chip shops... a travelling European circus out in the new car park, a girl crossing the high-wire without a safety net, oblivious to the fact that she can see the houses of all my friends...

And then when I was ten, and long since given up on subtitling the news, an event I scarcely noticed at the time: the transfer of all of the country's political prisoners to Portlaoise, effectively making the two things one, the town and the prison, the prison and the town.

November, 1973: a bitterly cold winter of protest and shortages, strikes and arguments. And every time I passed it by—that grey limestone building, its spot-lit parapets bristling with barbed wire—I tried to imagine the men inside in their cramped, perishing slop-out cells, and the men on the walls guarding them, themselves half-perished up there no doubt, like gargoyles exhaling visible breath in one of the harshest winters we'd seen in a decade with, if we knew it, nothing but harsh winters ahead.

The Belfry

If you wanted to get high in Portlaoise about 1972 or '73 (and you were still only ten years old), you joined the altar boys. Someone said that, from the red-brick belfry of St. Peter and Paul's church—the town's periscope, as I used to think of it—you could see right inside of the prison, just a few hundred yards away. If they were out in the exercise yard, you might even see the prisoners themselves in their manacles and chains, in their grey two-piece suits with the black arrows pointing to their heads, the way they did in comic strips. It was a fascinating idea, that the biggest mystery in our town—in our world—back then could be exposed, even partially, by simply climbing up into the belfry of the church.

And because everyone wanted to see inside the prison, everyone wanted to be an altar boy.

And so, the day the little puppet-frail parish priest came into our national school, and made his tour of the classrooms, talking to himself in that whispery, sibilant way he had, playing with his hands in the manner of someone delicately untying a knot, I forced to the back of my mind the image of myself dressed like something from a Christmas card, and instead concentrated hard on the possible view of the town, my town, that would spread out below me. And, like most of my friends in the classroom, I put up my hand.

Somehow, as we sat there with the blood draining first from our fingers, then from our wrists—so that we had to draft in our left arms to help hold the rights ones up—somehow we managed to force to the back of our minds the thought of all the early mornings and late evenings that lay ahead of us, all the hanging around outside and waiting, at funerals especially, among upset people, all that traipsing to and fro between the overheated vestry and the ice-cold church, as our brothers and fathers and fathers before them, had done.

And the truth was, yes, there were cold evenings, and colder mornings. But the belfry of St. Peter and Paul's was worth it. From the second- or third-floor windows of its concrete, red brick-encrusted tower, you could see a town that was breathtaking, captivating and, if you were like me and suffered a little from vertigo, dizzyingly so.

You could see Main Street, the lower part at least, starting its gradual rise and swing up away from the not-yet overgrown Triogue river, still alive with pinkeens.

You could see, running up through what had once been our back garden and was now picked out by two lines of sulphurous yellow lights, the great four-lane curve of the town bypass, the link road as it was euphemistically known.

You could see Rankin's Wood to your left, the bloated crowns of the trees obscuring their trunks and branches below so that the whole wood looked like a single entity—which it was—a living creature even then struggling to survive at the edge of an expanding town.

And over to your right, out the opposite window, you could see the Burial or Burying Ridge, one of the town's oldest cemeteries, changing shades of green as its long grass was blown this way and that, as if the spirits of all those buried here—the Phelans of Grattan Street, the Kellys of Courtwood, the Bergins of Woodbrook, the Lalors of Eyne—and of all the mellifluously named townsfolk laid to rest in the town—the Pattinsons and Merediths, the Grinlintons and Knags—had never quite gone to sleep.

On a cold funeral evening, you might be stood in the cross-winds of that belfry for twenty minutes or half an hour, watching out for the first sighting of the hearse and cortège on their way in from the hospital. But once the polished chrome and hood of the hearse came into sight, all thoughts of the cold disappeared and it was time to approach the bell.

And if you were lucky, and one of the older boys was too busy smoking, or was down somewhere outside the church chatting to some young one, you could grasp that huge, barely flexible rope that hung down through the middle of the bell shaft, lean out over it to draw down with what little weight you had, then relax on the slight recoil to draw down even harder at its apex, over and over, feeling the pull of the bell and getting a sense of the rhythm, taking the weight and measure of it, the way someone digging turf has to, or someone digging a grave; until, with no effort whatsoever, and no resistance, suddenly you're in the air, lifted off the flat lifeless concrete surface your feet have been gummed to for the last twenty minutes, to have everybody else now suddenly below you, shouting up and laughing, and urging you on, to 'look at the prison, can you see the prison?', and you just clinging on and willing the next flight higher, soaring above yourself, the town, the world, in a literally ecstatic, almost religious moment, in which you understand at last the real meaning, the real significance of the word belfry. The bell. Free.

Don't They Look Gorgeous?

Being an altar boy was all about dressing up and looking holy. If your soutane or cassock was sufficiently long that, when you walked, you could make it look as if you were floating, that was better still. For those of us who would go on to take up karate in the County Hotel on Wednesday nights, all the bowing and expressionless standing around that serving mass involved would have its benefits. It was as if we were trainee Jedi knights (before *Star Wars* existed) or Shaolin monks who might, at any time, leave down their little bells and bowls and baubles and smack you in the face. If we had been singled out as prospective priests, the choice was random: for there were lads in the force who, had they not occasionally coughed or groaned or burped—or worse—showed no more signs of an inner life than some of the surrounding statues gazing blankly down.

"Don't they look gorgeous?" you'd hear, at least once a week, some old one say. But there was little consolation in that, this being the generation that had inflicted dickie bows on us a few years earlier.

Admittedly there were moments when the atmosphere of a particular service or church building (the few times we got to 'play away') got the upper hand. On those rare occasions even the more cynical and impatient of the monochrome foot soldiers could seem for a moment almost angelic. For the most part, however, for the majority of us it was a struggle to get through the consecration without either yawning loudly or, as happened at least once, making for the cruets but tumbling head-first over the grow-spurted legs of the sainted boy-child kneeling to your left or right.

In the mid 1970s, of course, the 'job' of altar boy was as yet open only to young males. Hence the appellation. Back then, with more or less everything at the time being segregated, this didn't seem especially odd. Indeed, from the day of our First Communion, when the boys found themselves installed in the pews on the right-hand side of the church, the girls on the left, despite ourselves we always sensed a kind of psychic, just-about-perceptible wall screening off that left side of the building; and to go there to gather up discarded mass leaflets, or to retrieve some old lady's forgotten hard-backed missal was to enter a foreign world, to venture across, quite literally, the gender divide.

And what made that journey all the more strange, of course, was the gender-bending, cross-dressing clobber we were dolled up in, for whatever reason, hand-made for each of us by a legion of Marys and Annes on Singer sewing machines spread throughout the land—the unsung heroes, the real driving force and engine, the cottage industry that was the Irish Catholic Church in its odd-as-all-get-out, bordering-on-the-pagan, *Hail Glorious St. Patrick,* hard-to-believe-it-now heyday.

Fr Browne and the Dimension
of the Present Moment*

Old people have a habit of turning into birds. It seems true so often that it must be an unwritten rule of growing old. The broad-hipped woman who ran the little grocery and sweet shop in the middle of Main Street when I was a child transformed, gradually, into a warm, cooing, contented little hen as the years passed, towards the end rarely moving from her roost at the front window from which she watched the world go by.

Another old man who always drank in one of the pubs across the street transformed into a kind of raven, blackening into age, hardening, sharpening, becoming so alarmingly thin that, as a boy, I was always afraid when passing him on the street that I might knock against him and cause him to collapse into a pile of bones and clothing, like one of the pretend scarecrows we made with old clothes and clothes-hangers and then knocked down with stones in the farthest reaches of our long back yard.

Where another old neighbour had formerly looked on the world with vague amusement and a permanent half-grin, now he appeared constantly to monitor and scan the street with a razor-like eye, as if danger was ever just a matter of feet away.

And at the lower end of the street, the handsome old publican became almost stork-like in old age, while his near neighbours— an elderly husband and wife—once full of chat it was said, in their retirement became puzzled and cautious as owls.

But behind such startling outward transformation came, in many cases, a more gradual but far more troubling inward exchange of identity and role. For some it was dementia; for others, like my father, it was Alzheimer's; for others it was simply age making some obscure point.

In the case of our aged Parish Priest, the Very Rev Fr Browne, when age began to erase his past, cruelly it provided him with a second copy of the present in its stead. For as his retirement in 1975 approached, this small, utterly bird-like man became, before the eyes of his parishioners, a martyr to memory.

Perhaps the clues were there from early on, in the pecking repetitions of his movements, the impression he often gave that his attention was somewhere else. And yet these are also the common signs of concentration, of an individual's power to enter into a kind of—or, in his case, distinctly—spiritual zone.

It took, therefore, quite some time before his behaviour was recognised for what it was, an orderly thrashing to stay upright in the relentless current of the present moment.

The loneliness of the church is legendary, from the humble sacristan about his rounds in the late evening to the whispering penitents in the dark confessionals, to the mute undertakers drawing up, briefly, bowing their heads, drawing away again. Good priests undoubtedly console themselves with the ultimate loneliness of the one in whose name the church convenes; but this scarcely heals the wound of their loneliness. And in the morning sacristy, with the altar boys whispering and joking in the next small room, the preparing priest has only tradition to guide him, routine to cling to as he makes his way into the world.

It was in that very emergence into the world that Fr. Browne's problem revealed itself. For just as my fellow altar boys and myself could sense an invisible screen or wall dividing the church down the centre, so too did Fr Browne seem to encounter a similar boundary the moment he came out from behind the physical wall that separated the Sacristy from the body of the church itself.

And so, on those bitter winter mornings when, somehow, we were up to serve mass for him before school (often even before having our breakfasts!), he would come out on the altar, genuflect sombrely and mount the two small runs of steps to take his place. Sometimes when he found himself having reverted unconsciously to pre-Vatican II, Tridentine fashion—back to the congregation—there would follow a small amount of fumbling about, or 'stage business', after which he would make his way back around the huge marble altar, to face the congregation, and raising his featherless wings of arms would invoke the Trinity in a voice made even more sibilant by the vagaries of a too-loud PA system in a cavernous, mostly empty church.

The mass itself was invariably long, and always felt longer at that hour of the morning, our stomachs grumbling, our attention wandering more than ever to thoughts of warm milk on Sugar Smacks, fried eggs weeping into fresh white toast. The congregation—a dozen people at most in a building that could accommodate perhaps a thousand—was mostly made up of guards and prison officers (warders, as they always were to us), themselves clock-watching in order not to miss the commencement of the next shift.

But miss it they often must have done, as we altar decorations often had to miss our breakfasts and run to school for fear of being late. For though Fr. Browne would bow, and bless himself, and raise his hands and bless us all at the end of mass; and though he would nod to us then stand and wait until we were there with him, ready to process together, back to the sacristy out of which we had earlier emerged—as soon as we were back behind that screening wall, some synapse in his mind would misfire and he would see himself as having just stepped out, as being on the way to mass and not on the journey home.

And before we might stop him (as if we kids *could* have stopped him), and with all of us in still in tow, little chicks in his wake, he would be heading back out again, to start again all over, the shock and horror on our faces only surpassed by the shock and horror on the faces of the prison officers and guards who in that moment had stood to cross themselves and leave, but were now utterly unable to bring themselves to do so—"In the name of the Father, and of the Son, and of the Holy Spirit…"—as if the cyclic nature of time (which idea had often crossed their minds, no doubt) was now a reality that could no longer be denied.

The Strap

Like a Christian Brother of old, my father kept a leather strap, and was known to use it. It was not enough simply to use a strap, in the confines and privacy of one's home: it was necessary to be known to use it, the power being as much in the threat as in the application.

More of a belt than the apparently custom-made straps the Irish Christian Brothers liked to carry, wide and undulating as the tongue of a cow, my father's strap was, I recall, about 9 inches long and made of a flat leather band, folded over onto itself lengthwise, then sewn along the length so that there was a slight but distinct seam down the middle.

Seam side up or seam side down, my father's strap, when it bore down on your fingers, left your hand on fire, your eyes on fire, and terrible confusion in your heart. For it was clear all along that my father loved us, even us three boys for whom the leather strap was all too often taken down from the shelf where it rested between the scissors and combs, the string and sticking plasters, to be removed from its double-strength elastic band and allowed to unfurl itself like, I always thought, the serpent in the garden of Eden.

To be fair to him, my father had grown up in a different time, a time in which such forms of discipline were not uncommon and where, if you were not receiving corporal punishment at home, you were almost certainly receiving it at school. My father's generation had a war in common, and childhoods of scarcity and hardship in which men disciplined their sons the way a farmer might a beast who had strayed off the path. There were crude and sometimes cruel solutions to problems that ought to have been solved in other ways.

And yet, incredible as it seems to me now, for a long number of years my father's strap was wielded in our house, and many evenings I sat there in the Breakfast Room, squeezing a still-burning hand, and gazing out at Main Street through the lace curtains that might as well have been steel bars.

And there must have been shame in the beatings too, for my father and for us, because I remember how dark a thing it felt to tell it to a friend one day in school (would we have been 8 or 9 or 10?), a friend who confessed to me that his father did it too, but preferring a stick or his open hand, and once in a while his fist... Sucking gobstoppers, in the bicycle shed, it suddenly became clear to us that we were very likely a whole school, a whole generation of young lads, being routinely beaten, and beaten down, for no real reason, and with no real purpose, and little chance of it coming to an end. The strange thing was that it was nearly always the beatings, the straps and the sticks themselves which were the enemy. Only when a school friend swore revenge on his father, and looked as if he meant it, did it dawn on us that the solution to such a widespread problem lay in individual, particularised action.

So it happened that one day, long enough after such a beating to be calm and clear about how to proceed, my younger brother and I decided to destroy my father's strap. We simply made up our minds that this particular chapter of our lives had come to an end. The details are sketchy, but I do recall that Sesame Street was playing on the television upstairs as we made our way down to the kitchen, hearing the fifth last and the third last stairboard creak as they had since we were born. By chance, my father was away somewhere, perhaps gone to a nearby town on business, and, despite the warning "He'll miss it!" from our mother who had always been horrified by its sight, I stood on a chair and took it from its resting place.

My brother, as I recall it, opened the front door of the range, and, holding the strap in the tongs from the open fireplace upstairs, I lifted it inside, this black coil of darkness, this leather, hand-held weapon of domestic terror. And we stood and watched it for a minute or two, twitch and straighten, spark and twitch, rise and snap and spark again, until the flames at last took hold of it and bathed in the sheer heat of the moment we shut the door of hell on it and moved well back.

All lives, simple or complicated, are full of mysteries. One from my own is how did our father react when he found his leather strap had vanished? For apart from looking for it, and threatening now and then to get another—which he never did—he never asked us directly if we had taken it or what precisely had become of it.

As if he knew. As if maybe he'd needed to have the decision made for him. As if it had long been clear, even to him, that the strap's time, if ever it had one, was long since gone. Soon his sons would be young men, his daughters young women. He and his wife would be a late-middle-aged couple growing old in patterns they had built around themselves.

And in the midst of all this change, at its mercy one might say, sometimes letting go turns out to be a kind of blessing. For without his leather strap my father's own beautiful hands, even while ours visibly toughened, slowly softened again.

'Papa Oom Mow Mow'

By the time I was 12 or 13 on most Saturday afternoons I was to be found, together with my brother or sister or one of my friends, in Bertie Black's on Lower Main Street, pouring over the list of the Top 40 or Top 100 singles which Mrs Black would have taped over the glass-topped display near the till, the handful of singles in stock in the shop ticked off with a blue pen to stop us from asking for others: "Do you have No. 9? No. 10? No. 11? What about No.12?"

Some days, of course, there would be such a flurry of teenage and pre-teenage activity around the counter that it was impossible to see what might have been indicated on the list, and so above the thrum and throng of discussion and argument (and the country music playing somewhere out the back) we called out anyway: "Do you have No. 9? No. 10? No. 11? What about No.12?"

Being myself the son of a sometimes beleaguered shopkeeper, I had some sympathy for the Blacks whose shop, like so many back then, was almost impossible to define, a place that stocked a wondrous, nay bewildering range of goods for sale, from sports equipment to toys and LPs, from women's jewellery to a particularly gaudy line in household goods. If one wanted the latest record by Joe Dolan or, for an aging aunt, a copy of *Among My Souvenirs* by the town's own Peggy Dell; if one had need of a gold-plated candelabra (the original of which Liberace might have owned); if what was missing from one's life was a tube of tennis, golf or ping-pong balls or a cast-iron Batmobile with a red plastic flame that poked out at the rear end when the back wheels turned, then Bertie Black's of Main Street was the place to go.

The fact that we were playing whatever few records we could actually afford on what must have been the cheapest record player in town—a mono, suitcase-sized chipboard job covered with blue vinyl held in place by fake gold studs—meant that as often as not our new treasures would skip, Gary Glitter hiccupped one time too many on 'If I Would I Could' and the siren at the beginning of 'Blockbuster' by The Sweet went on and on and on, as if unknown to us all just then someone had just blown a hole in the prison wall.

Of course we would put this down to faulty goods and, suitably incensed, would march back down to Black's, platters of scratched vinyl in hand.

These return trips were seldom satisfactory, of course, because the records when tested usually turned out to be fine, and on the rare occasions when we did manage to secure replacements they were unlikely to produce different results on our creaking old machine.

Quickly, though, we began to realise—my brothers, sisters, friends and myself—that there were other attractions in going down to Black's apart from to seek satisfaction. For behind the counter on the wall, the son Ken (or so we guessed)—like myself a decade later trying to improve my own father's behind-the-times business sense—had installed on the premises a gadget that would take them, in a flash, from the primitive conditions of the early 1970s into the late 1970s' brave new world: a two-way radio that connected downstairs and up, the public street-front shop with the inner private chamber of the place.

Now, whether it was Mrs Black herself who was at the counter or, as it often was, young Ken himself, the confusion that we record-toting, pop-music-quoting giddy teenagers brought in on a quest was almost sure to have the one call to the other looking for some news, some advice or help. And it was the ensuing communication that was always sure to reduce us to sniggering wrecks.

Click. "Black One to Black Two, do you read me, mammy, over?" *Click.*

Cuhhhh (*Cuhhhh* being the sound of static before and after ever communication from above). "Black Two to Black One." Then the almost deafening sound of Mrs Black clearing her throat. *Cuhhhh.* "What is it, Kenny?" *Cuhhhh.* "Over?" *Cuhhhh.*

Click. "Mammy, do we have a single by the name of 'Papa Oom Mow Mow' by Gary Glitter? Over." *Click.*

Cuhhhh. "Papa who?" *Cuhhhh.*

Click. "...Mow Mow. 'Papa Oom Mow Mow'. Over..." *Click.*

"Or," I'd try to interject, helpfully. "If you don't have that I might be interested in..." my eye rolling up and down the list in search of something even better...

Cuhhhh, Click. Click, Cuhhhh. Cuhhhhhhhh. "Mammy, can you hear me—is this thing working at all?"

"What about this one by Slade," I say.

"Which one's that?" he says, only half paying attention.

Click. Cuhhhhhhhhhh... Cuhhhhhhhhhh... Click.

"'Mama'," I offer, "'Weer All Crazee Now'."

Library Visits

1. The Highwayman

A highwayman by the name of Jeremiah 'Ger' Grant was the last man to be hanged in Maryborough, his execution in August 1816 taking place on the street outside the old gaol, afterwards the County Library, and now the Dunamaise Theatre, and so close to our house that, had someone been looking out at the time, they would have had a clear view of the spectacle.

In the way that I myself saw prisoners led into and out of the courthouse over the two decades I lived opposite on Main Street, an 1816 observer would have seen an uncommonly tall man (6' 1"), handsome (so they say), with short black hair, deprived of his sight by a blindfold, led up the steps of a free-standing stair which, subsequent to his being dressed in a noose, was kicked from under his feet, thereby snapping his neck.

The precise details and sequence of events I cannot substantiate, but this is how I've seen it for more than thirty years as it plays in my mind's eye. And as he swings there in his sweat-stained shirt and piss-stained britches, a cheer rings up from the enormous and appreciative crowd who have come from all over the country to see a man die.

Grand trials and executions were once so popular in Maryborough that in effect they became additional fair days, bands marching through Main Street, an atmosphere of carnival and celebration that, in its own way, would have been good for family business. When the famous Moore the Murderer was sentenced there in 1873, for instance, the turn-out was so enormous, and passions ran so high, that he had to be taken into court, like Hannibal Lecter, in a steel cage.

In the year or so before his own arrest, Jeremiah Grant, who came from Moyne in Tipperary, had become infamous on the highways and by-ways of the midlands as one of the most persistent of a veritable army of petty thieves then roaming the land. It could only have been a matter of time before he'd pay the price.

Raised by an uncle after the death of his father, Grant had been a successful farmer, a young married man and father of seven. In fact, at a time when so many smallholdings were threatened with failure, it was his determined effort to better his lot that attracted the attentions of a greedy landlord, one Gilbert Maher (whose son Nicholas, in a dangerous complication, would take up with Grant's sister).

There followed an attempted confiscation of a portion of Grant's goods and properties (among them various animals, a number of beehives managed by his wife...) upon which affront Grant unwisely brandished what was said to be a loaded pistol. Though the pistol was not discharged (presuming of course it had been in mechanical order), the damage had most certainly been done. The very sight of the firearm resulted in accusations of attempted murder, whisperings of Grant's possible connections to a variety of subversive groups, and in due course condemned him to a life on the run.

In the meantime, there was the liaison between his sister and the landlord's son. Convinced that Maher must have taken advantage of the girl, Grant and his brother John set out to exact their revenge. At first Mary resisted their help, even having them arrested; but later she repented, turned on her lover and beat out his brains with a rock.

Unsurprisingly, she went to the gallows. Her brother John was transported to Australia. And Jeremiah found himself locked up yet again. Over the following years he was seldom out of jail.

In Thurles one time he almost escaped but was overpowered by a jailer's assistant (female) and recaptured.

In Clonmel he once managed to saw through the bars of his cell and somehow freed the entire inmate population. On this occasion only Grant managed to remain at large, taking to the same local river that according to legend began to flow on the night on which Conn of the Hundred Battles had come into the world. Perhaps at last Jeremiah Grant was in tune with his fate: his own hundred battles behind him and going at last with the flow.

The story might and should have ended there. But not known for keeping his head down, within days Grant was rearrested and promptly taken to Maryborough Gaol. This time the escape bid was straight out of some bad cowboy movie: in his breakfast kipper a skeleton key hidden among the bones.

Whatever the truth of the story, the escape would be followed by his last hurray: his last round of hiding in ditches and woodlands; of sleeping in barns and safe houses through the locality; of emerging from nowhere to accost solitary travellers, never knowing if they might be better armed than was he.

Within a year, as might have been predicted, Jeremiah Grant was back behind bars again. And not just again, not just once more, but for the final time.

2. The Reference Room

The reference book spines with their bar-like appearance, their keep-out blank expressions, their burden of facts, claims and counterclaims gave the small room they filled its atmosphere of suppressed argument, its distinctly troubled air... Despite the friendly attentions of the members of staff—Cait Kavanagh, Patricia Lynch and Marguerite Gibson among them—even the adults I saw introduced into that small room looked like they were being lead into a cell.

At the far end of the Library, in the Children's Section, we devoured everything from *The Cat in the Hat* to a dozen identical Biggles books, pausing for *Make Your Own Cowboy Suit* or one of those *Teach Yourself Magic* books every mother's heart must sink to see, our home-made wands and packs of cards so woefully warped and clumsily marked that only the most indulgent parent could manage to applaud.

And yet even for us the Reference Room held some allure.

In a newspaper interview from 1966, the retired County Librarian Miss Helen Roe looked back on her years working in Portlaoise (during which time, as it happens, she was a friend of my mother's Aunt Kitt).

"I spent," she recalls, "14 years in the condemned cell in the old jail," after which the author of the piece explains: "The condemned cell happened to be her office during the years she was librarian there."

The fact that the office in question was not the Reference Room as I had imagined but a room above it on the first floor takes nothing from the discovery. For the notion that a library might itself be a kind of gaol, a kind of prison for ideas, was one I'd long since considered and was glad now to see reflected in the thoughts of someone else. For anyone who loves books, who has noticed the silences they accumulate, will know the truth of the comparison.

Even so it is remarkable to think of Miss Helen Roe back there before my time, and of all the Librarians and staff who came after her, in that condemned cell and those doubly haunted rooms, on the wall outside of which a gallows bracket had once been fixed so that a condemned man might swing in the street below.

Even the language of writing and books seems to hint at a connection with death and execution: *capital* letters (like *capital punishment*); *widows and orphans; hanging indents; body text and broken spines; bleed and layout; perfect binding; linen finish…*

And, almost two hundred years after the death of Jeremiah Grant, and of the twenty-one other prisoners executed there, one evening in the new theatre on the site of the old Library, on the site of old Maryborough Gaol, one last all-too appropriate printing term comes to mind: 'Ghosting', defined in the trade as the phenomenon of a faint image appearing on a printed sheet where no such image is intended.

3. The Bees, Again

For some reason, while sketching out this piece, I find myself thinking again and again about Ger Grant's wife and the beehives taken from her by their landlord. It was of course that original theft that set off the terrible sequence of events that became Grant's life, and death, not to mention the deaths of his co-accused, Carrol Whelan and a farmer from Ballinakill by the name of Michael Fanning who, when arrested, had in his possession a plate which the highwayman had stolen somewhere and which proved to be more valuable than his life.

I find myself thinking of the bees that used to come into our big, half-wild back garden on the opposite side of Main Street, in the second half of the 1960s, and long before then, before I was ever born. I remember the bee sting my sister got on her neck one day as a small child, and the huge swelling it raised within seconds inside of her flesh. I think of the bees and wasps my mother would catch on the back window, in half-full jars of water, the lips of which she'd daubed with orange marmalade.

In Portlaoise for a single night for a poetry event some years ago, I read an early poem of mine, 'For a Beekeeper', written in memory of the father of one of my friends, Anne Merriman, herself since tragically lost... The ghosting effect complicating and multiplied...

Somehow everything is connected to everything else. What other conclusion can we come to about this life? Captain Ger Grant I have only recently learned is buried in the gated graveyard of the old St. Peter's Church on Railway Street, barely a hundred yards from the front door of our old house.

And yet it was under that canopy of whispering leaves, where every autumn the sycamore seeds drift slowly to earth in their spellbinding whirligig motion, that I made one day what remains my only sighting of a swarm of bees. Perhaps there was a nest of them in there somewhere, at the rear of Fitzgibbon's house, or in the overgrown ivy that binds up the centuries-old ruin. Or perhaps like me they were just passing by—in their case, passing over—the high stone walls or filtering through the chained-up gates, almost ghost-like and oblivious to all human obstacles, the perfect symbols, as the ancients realised, of immortality.

Everlasting Light

As the townie kids of a rural-born father, before we even made it into our teens we'd seen more changes than he'd anticipated in his entire life.

Not all of them were for the better.

The old valve radio high on the kitchen shelf was replaced by various portable transistors, none of which he could ever find when he needed one—though they were the perfect size for our covert, i.e. underneath the covers, night-time listening.

The wonderfully efficient dynamos on bicycles he'd seen replaced by pointless battery lamps, and his beloved Sam Smile blades were taken off the market to be replaced by six-pack bags of plastic razors which, despite being labelled disposable, he could never throw away.

This was the era, we were discovering, of planned obsolescence, when the big companies my parents had grown up with—and grown up respecting—began to build their products to fail.

We talked about it in school and at home during meal times, laughing at the notion of it, frightened that we couldn't understand the point. If we were the ones buying things, shouldn't the things we bought be made the way we wanted them to be? Hard-wearing, long-lasting, reliable and cheap.

As the waves of plastic tat increased through the 1970s, and just as we were fearing for our survival in the mountains of patched-up white goods and broken-down toys, about 1975 or '6 we stumbled upon the greatest miracle of all. On sale in Peter

Rice's in the Market Square (perhaps elsewhere too), available in maybe half a dozen brightly-coloured one-piece plastic cases, as if delivered to us direct from the future, for one pound and fifty pence an Everlasting Flashlight might be ours and, for once and for all, break the bonds of our enslavement to shoddy craftsmanship.

What precisely might be inside of those pastel-coloured cases we never stopped to think, if only because, like primitive natives, we knew we could not hope to understand.

All we knew about power was that to make it one had to consume or harness something else. Cars burned petrol, the ESB generating station outside Portarlington burned turf. Our geography book said there was a station on the Shannon that made its power from the flow of the river, but with so few big rivers, and bog all around us, burning would be good enough for us. Some countries had nuclear power, but mostly they were the ones that were big enough to build the stations—and bury the waste—near the homes of someone else.

That none of this knowledge clarified what might be going on inside those Everlasting Flashlights only amplified their attraction for us.

In our relative innocence what we did not consider was that anyone might try to sell, openly at least, anything that was not all it was made out to be. No doubt Peter Rice who demonstrated and sold them to us enthusiastically (in a shop that was overflowing with such wonders) himself had taken to this latest product in the belief that he was acting as a conduit between the population of the town and the bright future it so richly deserved.

And so with pleas and beggings and promises we did the rounds of parents, piggy banks and bottle return shops (up to 5p on a large bottle of Fanta or Coca Cola) until we had enough for a flashlight each, which we duly purchased and set up in three locations about the house and turned on.

And the light they gave was truly special, truly magnificent.

Until, after about an hour and a half, first one, then the second and shortly afterwards the third gave up the ghost.

There is a persistent story from south Tipperary that, during the laying of the Kinsale Gas pipeline about a decade later, a small farmer bribed some of the pipeline workforce to run a secret supply to his homestead, a considerable sum of cash money changing hands. When the gas suddenly ran dry some time later, and with the work gang long since moved on, the farmer did the only thing he could, dug up his yard to follow the pipe to the break he expected to find. Instead, just a few yards from his house, but out of sight in a dip in the road, he unearthed an empty canister of a well-known brand of household gas.

Similarly, knowing there was no point in going back, the harsh lesson of the incident becoming clear to us, some time that night we took apart those Everlasting Flashlights, resorting to hammers when screwdrivers failed to gain ingress. Inside, surprise surprise, cradled between a spring and the nipple of an ordinary bulb, was a two-barrel battery bearing Chinese print, like a miniature nuclear power station after all the workers have found sense and walked away for good.

Balls

If you were not as thick as two short planks, your pants were not on fire or your tail (the taunt assumed you had one) was not like a telephone wire, you could briefly feel normal, invisible even, in the primary school yard during break-time.

Here, marbles were the preferred distraction and chosen item of veneration, and the occult rules of 'Dandies' (in essence, hit the last one rolled), 'Eye-drops' (vertical bombardment) and 'Closest to the Wall' (self-explanatory) were enough to keep half a dozen schoolboys in heated argument for fifteen minutes until a nun appeared in a doorway, like a figure from a cuckoo clock, to stir the air with her wooden-handled bell.

'Torpedoes', a game of my own invention, and an exciting one to boot, inexplicably was never popular. Perhaps it borrowed too liberally from a number of others with better pedigrees. Perhaps its dependence on empty toilet rolls to guide projectiles to their target was too much of a reminder of earlier toilet embarrassments for my short-trousered, ankle-socked but all-grown-up-now classmates. As research and development facilities, playgrounds employ strict quality control.

When we were not on our knees, scrambling after marbles like so many mythological giants over a landscape of eyeballs, we were obsessed (being the age we were) with whatever might fit in our mouths and had the most passing resemblance to food. Inflating and popping 'chaing gaing' or chewing gum without getting it all over your face was a standard warm-up exercise, following which one might nurse (for hours on end) a giant multicoloured gob stopper (at regular intervals to be taken out and measured or shown to admiring friends, if only to flex the jaw muscles and lips), or pour a kind of lumpy pink powder onto one's tongue (more gritty than sherbet) and wait, grimacing, for the spittle thereon to ignite. What *was* that stuff? Could it really have been legal? How well I remember those headaches.

Though for the most part harmless, the youthful fascination with putting things in mouths of course inevitably lead to the occasional serious problem. Apart from the close call of my own with a small whistle, there was also an episode where my older brother, no more than a tot himself at the time, was saved from certain choking by a quick-witted and slightly older neighbour, Des Robinson, who lifted him off the ground, turned him upside-down and shook until the offending item—a marble, as I recall—rolled innocently away between their feet.

In the late 1960s and early 1970s, plastic footballs were still relatively uncommon, and the arrival of an even half-decent ball into the school yard was sure to attract a band of would-be Pelés and George Bests and result in at least one or two scuffles, a fair deal of name-calling ("You big daw," "You little squart") and displays of brilliance by Kevin Mitchell, Christy Cahill and a handful of others that left kids like me looking in the drains for marbles lost earlier in the week.

In the convent grounds, where we still mixed with but were mostly oblivious to girls, skipping ropes were of course used for skipping but as soon as they fell into the hands of a boy became any of a variety of weapons which included trip-wires, nooses and lassoes as well as the Portlaoise version of the South American bolas—a string with a ball at either end—at one time to be found dangling from every other power line that inscribed the skies above our heads.

And then, with the opening in 1973 of the Swedish-owned Tretorn factory in a field off the new bypass, the town, nay the whole county, was suddenly flooded with tennis balls—not the slightly hairy, interleaved twin-tongue, yellow flannel-swaddled version of same (which one might find but have to pay for in any sports shop now, or then in an open basket at the back of Bertie Black's down the way), but rather the as-yet uncoated and only crudely gummed-together raw-rubber, twin half-shell inner ball at the heart of same which, suffering from various small but happily fatal imperfections, had rolled off the assembly lines in their tens and hundreds and perhaps their thousands too, but by some grace of God or Swedish management were not destroyed or melted down to be used again but instead were leaked out into the local population, free and gratis, a yellow rain that was absorbed by our thirsty soil and out of which would grow a whole new enthusiasm for the game.

Love All

In the Portlaoise of the 1970s there were two tennis clubs. One was owned and run by the ESB as their staff social club: it was just at the then outer limits of the town, out the Abbeyleix Road and was open to the general public—the young lads of whom, like myself, gravitated to the pool tables in the club house, happy to watch their sisters and friends knock a handful of yellow tennis balls from the local factory back and forth, desultorily, until the sun went down.

The other tennis club, The Portlaoise Lawn Tennis Club, was a very different affair.

The Portlaoise Lawn Tennis Club was situated behind a small Protestant parish hall more or less in the centre of the town. Being located just opposite the wonderfully named Dead Wall—the biggest wall I'd seen in my life until then —gave it a kind of central authority. But if the Dead Wall had been built to hold up and back the weight of the thirty-foot railway embankment that runs through the town, the small lawn tennis club across the road from it was proof that gentler, more fragile activities could occupy the hearts and minds of the populace of the town.

In truth, I don't think I ever actually played what might be called a game of tennis, either in one of those two clubs back then, or elsewhere since. My mother in her time had often done so, and later both of my sisters regularly went out on summer evenings, tennis rackets in hand, to play at one of the tarmac courts that would later appear in the grounds of the Presentation Convent. Despite this, tennis remained for me an odd if oddly fascinating, game.

It was true that, unlike any other game I could think of, or saw anywhere around me, tennis alone broke the gender divide, which was a divide worth breaking, as far as I was concerned, and couples could often be seen playing together, even in Portlaoise. And it was even true that the championships at Wimbledon, and maybe even at other tournaments, had a category called Mixed Doubles, which was exactly that—as if, despite its apparent tameness and a dress code that gave it an *olde worlde* feel, tennis was at the same time somehow, discretely, revolutionary.

Yet the truth was that, in my age group at least, tennis was a girls' game, a game that us boys could watch, or pretend *not* to watch, but about which we were, as in so many other respects, in the dark. Surely there was more than meets the eye to a game in which the word 'love', not to mention the word 'match', was used over and over.

But boys simply did not play tennis. By which I suppose I mean Catholic boys. Where Gaelic footballers, soccer or rugby players of my acquaintance seemed intent on mucking up their kit as quickly as possible after the initial throw-in or kick-off, tennis players at the end of a match would come off the court in the same virginal whites as they'd gone out. It seemed to go against what games were all about, a kind of rough and tumble, a kind of letting go and giving in and going wild.

It took just a small incident one summer's night to change my mind about tennis and to see it less as some affected pastime of the gods, stopping to sip their ambrosia, and more as just another, if more stylised, version of a greater cosmic game.

Having spent the afternoon after school at a friend's house (where the main activities had been drinking Coca Cola and pillow-fighting in his elder brother's bedroom), this particular summer's evening I took a short cut back home up Railway Street, which meant I had to pass along by the side of the Dead Wall (looming up over me like a cliff face), and of course by the Portlaoise Lawn Tennis Club. And as it happened, whatever evening of the week it was, a Friday perhaps, a tennis club social was in full swing: some local tournament had concluded earlier in the day, and now disco music and the glow of flashing, coloured lights was spilling out of the high windows of the small hall.

It was then I noticed that the parked car beside which I was idly standing, half listening, half thinking of nothing at all, was moving from side to side and up and down. And, just as others in my class had claimed, though I hadn't believed them, when I stepped back, startled, and glanced over again, through the steamed-up windscreen I could just about make out two shapes, two figures, one female, one male, and both dressed in white, their arms wrapped tight around each other, for all the world like two angels struggling to be human again.

Going Underground: The Tunnels Of Portlaoise

From the time of its erection in 1548 almost until the day of its demolition just short of 300 years later in 1835, the Fort of Maryborough (under all of its various names) was seldom without attackers at its walls, brandishing swords, spears, flaming torches and copies of the Bible no doubt, among other things.

For the occupants of such a place, a secure keep and, just as important, a ready and ideally concealed secondary exit were paramount; without either, rather than being a place of sanctuary such a fort was more likely to become a place of slaughter.

Therefore, as in many other fortifications dating from the time, it is not unthinkable that the Maryborough fort would have had at least some rudimentary underground passageway leading from it to relative security some distance away.

In the case of Fort Protector the persistent story was that it and the town that grew up around it had been built on a series of underground passages—a veritable maze of them if some of the older townsfolk were to be believed. This of course fuelled the dreams of us schoolboys who were not much bothered by the lack of concrete evidence. Were there not, after all, those two or three houses in the middle of Main Street—Burke's Drapery almost directly opposite us among them—whose truly cavernous basements suggested a subterranean world that might have gone unexplored for centuries?

I took to the small press in our kitchen, built in under the main stairs, and from it pulled out half a dozen boxes of my mother's accumulated rags and tins of Brasso and various other polishes, but instead of a flight of stone stairs leading down into the bowels of the earth I found only a nest of spiders and mouse droppings that kept me from further exploring for a number of years.

Yet the rumours persisted. There was, some claimed to have heard at home, a tunnel that lead from the old fort to the very primary school we attended, and another that lead all the way out to Dunamase, a distance of a good three miles or more. Could it be true that, like the opening scene of some 1970s horror movie, we were studying our five times tables, seated in pairs above the yawning chasm of the town's greatest mystery?

Perhaps someone's parents had been speaking about it over dinner, having recourse to the four or five books and as many newspaper articles in which it had been mentioned over the years. But we soon learned that almost a century before, back in 1901, the then Parish Priest Rev Dr. Taylor had been summoned by a stonemason, Patsey Lynch, preparing to lay the foundation of new buildings in the Convent grounds when he had come upon an underground passage that he followed for hundreds of yards before it became too narrow and possibly dangerous for him to proceed. The PP, not seeing what else could be done, had ordered the tunnel sealed up with blocks.

Then in 1951 it was rediscovered, again during renovation work. And given that just twenty years had passed since then, it seemed entirely plausible that the tunnels might still be there. According to reports from that last occasion, the tunnel beneath the school had been seen to turn, as might be expected, back towards the late medieval fort up town, but the other end had led off in a direction that was at least consistent with the Dunamase theory, whatever about the distances involved.

On the occasion of this latest rediscovery, fears for the stability of the tunnels (by now, as well as extensive Convent buildings, a whole town had been built above-ground!) lead to their being blocked up after only the most cursory of inspections.

As recently as 1974, yet another suspected tunnel was discovered near the old St. Peter's burial ground, in the centre of the town (and within the perimeter of the original fort), raising yet again the possibility of an underground network, an invisible town, as I like to think of it, beneath our own.

But in 1974, in May of that year to be precise, it wasn't a suspected tunnel in St. Peter's but the discovery of a very real tunnel in the grounds of St. Fintan's Hospital (directly across the road from the prison) that would make the national news, and that would make of one of my class mates a kind of local hero.

In 1974 I was, and most of my friends were, 11 years of age, and 11-year-old boys have both an abundance of energy and a natural curiosity about the world that is almost pathological. Therefore when my class mate Joey Geoghegan, whose family then lived in the gate lodge of St. Fintan's hospital, invited a gang of us to go and explore with him the tunnel he had discovered in the hospital grounds (running under the Dublin Road itself, or so he claimed), at first I was tempted to go. Three of four of my friends had immediately declared they would be going. Why not me? Was it the prospect of having to crawl into some dark and filthy and maybe rat-infested place? (Even according to Joey himself, the tunnel was some kind of "half-stream or sewer"). The suggestion that we might enter it on "a raft" he had made (or had he found it? or did we have to build it still?) didn't seem to me—on that day at least—to promise much.

Years later, and unemployed, when I wondered if I might be cut out for journalism, my failure to go along on that excursion on that particular day would helpfully reminded me I am not. Even when Joey and my other classmates came back into school the following morning, enthusing and marvelling about their adventures underground (I was thinking, Huckleberry Finn meets the Hobbit meets Last of the Mohicans), there seemed to me nothing so special in their descriptions that I wished I had seen it for myself.

Until that July morning in 1974 when every newspaper in the country, every news bulletin on radio and television, was full of the discovery of Joey Geoghegan's tunnel, a tunnel that, very likely over weeks and months if not years, had been wending its way slowly towards a manhole in the prison's exercise yard. It had even gone under the houses of the prison officers themselves!

In November 1971, nine prisoners had escaped on rope ladders over the walls of Belfast's Crumlin Road Gaol. Two months later seven prisoners swam to freedom from the prison ship HMS Maidstone that was docked in Belfast Lough. That was in January: apart from anything else the water must have been perishing! And in October of that same year, another seven men had tunnelled their way out of the Curragh prison camp—using nothing but a plastic lampshade, a couple of chisels and a few plastic spoons. Prisons were for keeping people in (for some); for others they were for breaking out of. That fact was finally beginning to dawn on us.

Subsequent news stories would reveal that the tunnel was in fact an extension of an underground stream that ran through the grounds of St Fintan's, and that it had been discovered by the Garda by accident after they came upon some suspicious drawings in the possession of a local Republican at the time 'helping them in relation to a number of other enquiries'.

To complete the story, *The Nationalist* newspaper carried a photograph of two of the hospital staff, pointing into the mouth of the tunnel, and in its accompanying story told us again what Joey Geoghegan had discovered—and would have told anyone who would listen, but in less restrained tones—months before: "The river, which formed the major part of the tunnel, originates in the Downs area, going under the Stradbally Road and across the grounds of St. Fintan's Hospital. Close to the Dublin Road and in the gardens attached to St. Fintan's Hospital, the river surfaces for a short space to form a small fishpond. It was at this point where the river again goes underground and across under the Dublin Road that the tunnel began."

If the tunnel under the old Convent building was home, as the legend had it, to a ghostly piper, trapped inside for centuries and playing, some swear, the eerie strains of The Coolin, then the prison under St. Fintan's Hospital, the Dublin Road and (very nearly) the prison itself, will forever resound with the voice of a schoolboy saying, with justification, "I told you, I told you so".

Holy Water

A week or so after she died in May 1976, I met my school friend Kevin's mother in the west entrance of St. Peter & Paul's Church, standing by the holy water font opposite the door, shaking out her umbrella, slowly unpeeling her brown kid gloves.

"Oh hello, Paddy," she said on seeing me there, her small features framed by her familiar silk headscarf with the lucky horseshoe pattern.

"Hello, Mrs M_____," I replied, no doubt with a smile, the strangeness of the encounter somehow not striking me right away. For one thing, I'd always liked Mrs M_____, and appreciated the fact that, however busy she was, she never failed to let me know she liked my dropping by, approved of me as company for her son. For another thing, living as she did just opposite the church, it wasn't unusual to run into her out and about in that part of the town.

"How's your mam?" she enquired, as ever. To which I replied in the usual way, "She's well," remembering to add "thank you," while half-expecting her son to appear and drag me away to his bedroom to admire his latest consignment of Bruce Lee posters, sent by an older sibling from the far side of the world.

"Be sure to tell her I was asking for her," said Mrs M_____, reaching for the holy water font to bless herself.

I turned to look at the rain outside, already falling heavily enough to obscure Brown's shop across the road, the Burial Ridge that rises behind it, the two flashing orbs of the new zebra-crossing, making themselves seen, invisible, seen…

"Better go now. Bye, Mrs M_____," I said, taking a deep breath, pulling my windcheater tight and making a run for it.

Only then, wind and cold rain in my face, after the best part of a minute in her company, did I suddenly remember that Mrs M_____ was dead, that she'd died maybe two weeks before, that I'd walked behind her family in the funeral cortège...

Feeling as if I'd just woken up—as if I'd just fallen out of bed and come to my senses—I skidded to a halt in the rain and looked back.

Was that someone there, that shadow in the half-open doorway, the trail of wet footprints behind me leading to where she stood in a long, belted mackintosh with rain-darkened shoulders, a pearl of Holy Water glistening on her forehead, another on the tip of her outstretched index finger...

Psycho Killer

It was, I remember, my brother's classmate John Griffin who told the story to a number of school friends in the CBS Tower Hill one winter's morning in the late 1970s, though other names and locations have been suggested. The credibility of certain tales depends on the relationship between the central character and the listener, so it is not unusual to hear even mundane stories subtly transformed in order to appeal to the present listener.

Either way, as often happens, it was ultimately the grisly nature of the episode that assured it a life of its own and, by that evening, made it a major subject of discussion over the dinner tables of Portlaoise and perhaps outlying towns.

The events in question took place on a particularly grim winter's morning, rain falling, wind blowing in that horizontal, anti-human way that makes a mockery of umbrellas and all but the longest of rainproof coats.

Mrs Griffin (or Mrs Rigney, my brother now wonders) was driving back in to Portlaoise town that particular morning, having run an errand somewhere. Passing what was then still the County Hospital (a place where people of a certain age almost inevitably slow down), she noticed on the corner of the Block Road an old lady struggling to stay upright against the gale.

So, of course, she pulled over, rolled down the window on the passenger side and asked the lady if she would like a lift into town, a distance of about half a mile. Headscarf pulled in around her face, gabardine coat drawn tight around her ample bosom, collars up, umbrella like a throttled pterodactyl hanging inside out and limply by her side; and on the road by her feet a shopping bag, bulging with whatever essentials old ladies seem condemned to drag out into storms; here was a woman in need of help. The words "Thank you" mumbled or muttered, just within hearing, just above the volume of the wind, their oddly high-pitched, strangely eerie tone accepted in the moment as a sign of strain, which anyone, mother or not, would have heard and felt pity for.

The inside latch is lifted by Mrs X; the door is pulled open by the lady; and, after that bulging shopping bag is placed in on the floor at the passenger side, the owner's arm is briefly revealed: a fist the size and weight of a boxer's, a coat sleeve riding up on an arm black with masculine hair—and now that it is close enough to see, the hint of a five o'clock shadow on the half-exposed cheek framed by the headscarf... Out of sheer instinct, Mrs X releases the handbrake, wrestles the steering wheel, plunges the accelerator to the floor, the strange figure running along behind her now, arms raised, roars and screams drowned out by wind and rain...

Who would not have listened? Who could not see it? Mrs Griffin (or Mrs Rigney or his own mother) out there in the tempest, driving for her life?

Somehow keeping her head, one of our mothers had managed to escape, had reached across, even as the car sped up and she dared not look back, to pull the door shut, to whiz past St Fintan's, the prison, St. Peter and Paul's, then right past the Burying Ridge, left down Rigney's Hill (coincidence?), up Tower Hill past the school, right at the old Bank of Ireland, and home to the station-master's house beneath the Dead Wall, an address seemingly made for a story like this, for the film by now running in all of our heads.

And what had she avoided? Almost certainly gruesome death. For in that Pandora's bag when the Garda came to examine it, wrapped in women's underclothes (some said), or bloodstained newsprint (according to others), was a hatchet, the hatchet familiar from all those late-night horror films and those songs where mothers kill their children, or children kill their parents, or woodcutters arrive just in the nick of time, breaking down the door ...

In our house, the ham and bacon went cold, the custard turned gelatinous in the pot and the tea went grey as we stared into the distance wondering what it meant to find ourselves now in a town where such dark deeds were afoot, where sinister strangers had penetrated our defences and night's deep blanket could no longer keep us warm.

The next morning in Fortune's newsagents, Bradbury's cake shop, Kennedy's pharmacy and White's grocery, all of our mothers met each other and began to relate the terrible tale.

And Mrs Griffin laughed, and Mrs Rigney blushed, and Nancy Boran shook her head, and someone promised to tan her son's behind for having a big mouth.

But every word spoken acknowledged a kind of innocence in that schoolboy love of horror and celebrated the safety of the streets and back roads, the lanes and by-ways of the county. When real horror came, our mothers seemed to know—as mothers always do—probably there would be no special effects to accompany it. Neither would it require the arrival of an agent from outside.

Garryhinch

"We often travelled to Garryhinch for turf,
My mining town father and I..."

The two lines above are from an early poem I wrote that responded to something in the wider landscape of the midlands: the relationship between people and place.

Garryhinch is about 5 miles (7 km) west of Portarlington, just across the Offaly border. The name derives from the Irish *Garraí Inse* meaning Garden on the River Island, suggesting a magical spot where one might idle away an afternoon or half a lifetime.

But, for all its natural beauty, in the mid 1970s the Garryhinch woodlands became the site of something the opposite of beauty, and the wonder aroused by the event which took place there was the kind that is more correctly termed bewilderment.

In October 1976, the Troubles again came home to Portlaoise, or found their way out of the Invisible Prison and into all of our lives. In the ongoing monitoring of unoccupied houses around the country, a five-man team of local Garda including 24-year old Garda Michael Clerkin from Portarlington and Detectives Thomas Peters and Ben Thornton, both Portlaoise based, had gone around midday to a house at Garryhinch where routine searches around the exterior revealed nothing unusual or otherwise amiss.

It was only when Garda Clerkin decided to conduct an inspection of the interior, gaining access through a rear window so as to open the front door for his fellow officers, that events took a significantly darker turn. For the moment Thornton entered the house, there was a huge explosion and "the whole building went up". Detective Peters, whose wife had been my teacher in primary school, and whose daughter had been my classmate, lost his legs in the blast. Detective Garda Thornton, though also in the house with Clerkin, was spared the worst by being buried under rubble where he remained until members of the Garda and local people, who came running when they heard the blast, some time later dug him out.

Garda Inspector Peter Fitzpatrick, would later report to the inquest that, when he arrived at the site of the explosion shortly afterwards, he and other assisting officers spent some 20 minutes searching before they located a severed arm and hand, on one finger of which an initialled signet ring identified it as belonging to Garda Clerkin.

IRA all the way. Up the Provos. *Tiocfaidh ár Lá.* The graffiti grew thicker and thicker on the toilet walls and the walls at the back of the swimming pool where the older kids gathered to smoke and the younger ones to look on. Like barbed wire laid over barbed wire, it ceased now to have any meaning.

All I could think of was Garda Peters (whom I never knew, never met, but realised—as we all did—would likely suffer for the rest of his life). I thought about his daughter, hoping she would someone know how horrified and hurt we all were for her (too young and awkward and confused to find the words).

I thought too about my time in primary school, about Mrs Peters and all the teachers I had never met again but whose tales and myths and stories have stayed with me since: Labhraidh Loingseach, the king who had ass's ears; Br'er Rabbit out-smarting Br'er Fox, exploring the briarpatch down by the river or deep in the woods...

And I thought too of a schoolday nature walk she took us on one morning, some autumn woodland maybe only half as beautiful as Garryhinch, but where her descriptions of the flora

and the fauna, of things out in the open and things half-hidden,
like a kind of poetry filled us kids with awe.

Lourdes

When it came to earning a living my father, like the parish priest himself, was employed by God. The Irish missionary orders, for whom our pennies were collected in primary school and then sent off to their many foreign outposts, were cheered and admired for they work they did for the faith, bringing the light of Christianity to darkest Africa. Yet my father received no such tributes or accolades, though he laboured long into the night most nights on his own personal *via dolorso:* the organisation of the annual parish pilgrimage to Lourdes.

In 1858 the Blessed Virgin appeared no less than 18 times over a six-month period to a 14-year-old peasant girl at a grotto in the French Pyrenees. During the 1970s, responding to a now-growing demand occasioned by cheaper air travel, my father took on the task of organising the annual parish pilgrimage to that far-flung place. In itself this called for something of a second miracle, given his inherently disorganized nature and the inexperience of those who, like Chaucer's pilgrims, gathered about him looking for salvation and adventure in equal measure.

This was still in the days when the trophies of international travel were, for adults, a couple of cartons of King Size cigarettes, and for the kids an oversized Toblerone like something a pharaoh had conjured in a dream. These were the days when every young girl still wanted to be an air hostess in a pencil skirt, and every small boy wanted to be the pilot who flew her everywhere.

As far as I could understand from the conversation in my father's office, though the entire population of the town (and surrounding townlands) had already been to Lourdes, most of them were saving up again for the next expedition. Because my father operated a system whereby pilgrims could pay in instalments, the office—especially on Saturday mornings—was always full of little old ladies making that particular week's deposit of ten or five or sometimes even fewer pounds. Though not known within our house for his even temper, my father to be fair to him was always civil and welcoming to them all, even when the complex instalment plan taxed his rudimentary bookkeeping abilities to the point of breaking. Certainly there were days when he might have preferred to devote himself to other things: pointlessly shifting unsorted boxes of papers or washing down the front of the house in a tidal wave of suds, dressed (to our mortification) in an oversized raincoat and black sou'wester hat.

Mostly it was the older townsfolk who went, and older townsfolk therefore who gathered on those endless mornings in our Main Street 'shop' to discuss French weather or the terrors of French cuisine. It was far from ideal that the shop and our house (our kitchen in fact) were joined by a doorway (later closed up), and the drawn-out meetings would see my father dip in and out, taking his breakfast in equally drawn-out instalments.

One of everyone's greatest fears had to do with the hotel sharing arrangements in which, as if at random, my father might throw together a bemused local postman with two or more old dears, or double-book a bug-eyed comedian with the impeccably behaved local curate who'd struggle to find a polite way to let him know. A more enterprising soul might have seen the potential to establish a Portlaoise Pilgrimage and Wife-Swapping (or partner-swapping) Agency, but my father, alas, took it all very seriously and, like some South American holy statue, sweated blood over every smallest detail. All of it combined to make the build-up to the annual August pilgrimage the dominant tension of our childhood summers.

What could have gone wrong? Answer: everything.
Mosquitos, allergies, robberies, loss,
cuts and abrasions, sunburn, the trots;
falls in the restaurant, tumbles on the stairs,
in the candlelight procession, from a parked-up wheelchair;
bags going missing, hoteliers that shrugged
with Gallic indifference, stains on a rug;
and just over the border, and not going away,
the Basque separatist friends of the IRA...

Whatever profit my father made out of the annual expedition to Lourdes, a good part of it must have been eaten up in phone-calls to Dublin, seeking, on behalf of one pilgrim or other, reassurances on every conceivable detail of the accommodation, the itinerary and all related matters with the possible exception of the original miracle itself.

Even so, he stuck at it for years, for over a decade in fact.

"I want to be in with Mrs So-and-So not Mr Such-and-Such. Janey, Nicholas!" The delicious hint of scandal. None of them wanting to be in with Mrs X who talked all the time (and whose husband paid for her to go away every year, simply to be shot of her), or with Mr Y for that matter (whose feet stank and whose only luggage consisted of a plastic razor and a change of socks, the former in his breast pocket, the latter—with a copy of the *Farmer's Journal*—in a plastic bag he was seen to bring with him and, five days later, brought back home again).

In our family we still remember (fondly, fondly) the old lady who appeared one busy morning with a long handwritten list of her 'special dietary requirements' to be copied and sent ahead to her hotel. On my return five minutes later from Midland Stationery, she insisted on comparing her original with the photocopy, word by word and line by line, as though she imagined it had been made by a monkish scribe maintained by Jimmy Finn in a beehive hut somewhere out the back.

We remember too the scenes that would begin with a line like, "Now, Nicholas, I'm not at all sure about this, let me get out my glasses here..." followed by the sound of a bag spilled out on the counter, the contents to be prodded and poked at, commented on at length... Such a sound was a signal for one of us to put the kettle on, for my father to come out from behind his counter, to pull up a chair, then two (the first one for her, the second for himself), to switch on a second bar of the fluorescent light and the two-bar heater and, while he was at it, turn the key in the door—in the vain hope that there might be a miracle and this might be the last such search of the day.

"Nicholas, is this the same Hotel Majestic we were in two, or was it three, years ago? I thought my bed was too near to Mrs W's..."

"Nicholas, Mrs. G got three labels in her pouch and I only got the two!"

"Nicholas, I didn't use one of my labels last year! Can I use that this year even if it's not the same colour as last year's?"

"Nicholas, Nicholas, I didn't get any letter from the Spiritual Director in my pouch!"

It is just a week now to departure, and I am attending the preparatory meeting of the organizers and pilgrims in the vestry at the rear of St. Peter and Paul's, a meeting that invariably degenerates into chaos.

"Nicholas, I didn't get any letter from the Spiritual Director!" The sme voice, more strident this time.

My father, over the growing murmur of discontent and rumour, trying to maintain his composure against growing odds, spells it out for the umpteenth and final time.

"Ladies and gentlemen, fellow pilgrims," he loans a kind of presidential tone to the proceedings, "to clarify any concerns or questions you might have let me list out for you now" [we know it is coming] "what you should find in your *pooches—*"

My father's constant mispronunciation of the word 'pouch' is a matter of great hilarity to all of us, and whichever of us young Borans is forced to be present at this year's meeting will at least have one bright nugget to later bring back home to his or her waiting siblings.

Shoeboxes full of 'pooches' and tickets are passed around, mixed up, passed back, passed forth, passed back again. Laughter, anger, patient explanations. My father reads, for the umpteenth time—he says the words 'umpteenth time' for the umpteenth time—what seems by now almost a sacred list: "In no particular order—a map of Lourdes; a letter with the name, contact details and booking number of your hotel; a letter from myself; a letter from the Spiritual Director..." And on, and on.

And after all of the jumble has been sorted out, the priest heading home for a well-needed rest, and silence and strong whiskey or a watery cup of tea, my father dumps the paperwork in our small front room and makes his way across to Lewis's pub for a whiskey for himself and a nice cold pint, its head as white as the snow-capped Pyrenees.

And of the pilgrimage itself? Candlelight processions of limping thousands and wheelchaired thousands, in a river of flickering lights that would move the coldest heart. A day trip to Gavarnie or San Sebastián, my father at the front of the bus, re-interpreting the French interpreter's perfect English commentary: "Now just to repeat what Christine said there..." The whole busload of pilgrims shouting back as one: "Ah, Nicholas, would you ever shut up?" the cheap wine and August sun adding to the madness of it all.

For away from home, the mood could only improve. Laughter followed some small groups everywhere they went, and they did come back looking younger if not utterly transformed. Others were out, whenever the opportunity arose, on terrace bars toasting each other with raised glasses, saluting the ones who were heading off, for the third or fourth day in succession, to the ice-cold baths. "Imagine, this time tomorrow we'll be going back!" one young daughter was heard to marvel during one such gathering. To which her mother replied, apparently happy where she was: "Jaysus, B_____, I don't give a shite if we never go home!"

Aged fourteen I went for the first and only time and confess a lot of it was wasted on me. I bought a Bruce Lee T-shirt in a local market. Afterwards, without thinking, I wore it down to the grotto: the image on it, from the film *Enter the Dragon,* of a man stripped to the waist, scarred by assailants, doing anything but turning the other cheek.

Dress Code

At a time when British tabloids and the girls of Page 3 were still only beginning to appear in small-town newsagents, the only place hot-blooded teenagers and pre-teenagers could hope to encounter exposed female flesh was on the covers and in the impossibly glossy pages of the travel brochures that graced the counters and window displays of the town's two travel agencies, Dunne's LSA down the street and my father's own Airboran Travel.

Perhaps this is the reason why, almost every day of the week, clutches of lock-jawed school kids would turn up on our doorstep (boys vastly outnumbering girls), requesting brochure samples for some school geography project when, as was the case with myself, it was entirely a different kind of geography that was mostly on their minds.

True, the Coliseum Cinema on Bull Lane (and the not-long-closed Paul's on the Well Road) often boasted films with provocative titles, but the racy poster artwork was invariably expurgated by the cinema's manager Jimmy Ryan, sitting up late into the night (as we imagined him), thick black marker in hand as he attended to the modesty of Ursula Andress, Raquel Welch, the various Bond girls and countless brides of Dracula, closing an open shirt here or lowering a hemline there so that the town might not, that night at least, spontaneously combust with the heat of unrestricted passion.

The irony, of course, as with all censorship, was that the appearance of those same thick black marker lines and patches on a cinema poster succeeded only in suggesting more nudity than it might otherwise have been able to suggest—and more indeed than the film was likely to produce. Indeed, the posters became sought-after objects in themselves, and many a young fellow attempted to liberate one from the wooden and glass cases that were fixed to the outside wall of the cinema, one on either side of the door, though for the most part their locks repelled all but the most determined of young perverts.

In the late 70s I was still too young to even try to get permission to attend one of these dodgy "action" flicks that seemed to occupy so much of the discussion in the bicycle shed. And by the time I *was* old enough they seemed pretty much to have disappeared or been transformed into something else. Even so, like a handful of school friends I did wonder what secrets regular cinema-goers like 'Nobby' Styles, 'Killer' Collins and other significantly older lads were privy to in what had clearly become the new church for the town's dissenting youth—a cinema which, after all, had been named for the place where early the Christians were fed to the lions.

Two Scenes from the Short Career
of a Midlands Ninja

1976

Tall, thin, in his early 40s maybe, with a light thatch of curly hair on top, a boxer's flat nose, a pronounced jaw-line and scrawny, sinewy arms, the man who stood in front of us in the middle of the dance hall of the County Hotel looked more like an Irish farmer disturbed by noises in the night than any mental image of Bruce Lee any of us had.

Portlaoise Karate Club. Those of us who had seen the advert in the local newspaper, and instantly imagined some far eastern tiger coming to teach us how to fly, stared in open-mouthed disbelief. One or two adults tried to hide their disappointment by admiring the Japanese lettering on his long black belt, the crest on the back of his short-sleeved tunic, a dove wrapped around a fist.

But there was no getting away from the facts. Despite our week of heart-pounding dreams, our scurrying around to come up with karate suits—or anything that might pass for karate suits—we were nothing more than some raggle-taggle bunch of small-town townsfolk in bare feet on a bad night in a half-heated hall, less *Enter the Dragon* than *One Flew Over the Cuckoo's Nest*.

There was quite an amount of work ahead of us all.

1980

One of the things about teenage, and male teenage in particular, is that the flood of new hormonal energy racing through the veins often brings a sense of self-belief that has little to do with the external realities. The young men who poured out of the kung fufilms, and then injured themselves trying, like the Big Boss himself, to jump over parked cars are one example of it.

An example of my own also comes to mind and heralded for me, had I been paying attention, the end of my undistinguished martial arts career.

One evening talking to my mother as she cooked the evening meal, I recognised as if for the first time how much in recent years I had grown when measured beside her. That I also realised her present height was less than the height at which I could comfortably kick (thanks to five years of karate workouts) was a fact a more mature fighter would not have felt it necessary to prove.

"Ma," I said, "I have an idea. You stand there, and don't move an inch, and I'll swing my right foot right over your head."

The bacon sizzled on the pan, the eggs bubbled, tapped and hopped in the silver saucepan. What could my mother have possibly been thinking? What could I have been thinking?

"OK," she said, checking the clock, "but do it quick. I've got to cook the tea."

And that was that. Ridiculous as it seems now (even then, five seconds later), like a knife-thrower and his steely-eyed assistant we faced each other between the cooker and the back door, Thelma Mansfield watching from the cover of the *RTÉ Guide*.

I emptied my mind (not hard to do at the best of times), shifted my weight to my left foot and—swung out high.

Not, however, high enough.

A millisecond later we were both on our backsides on the floor, my mother's fall, mercifully, partly broken by the thick-brush doormat, my own (deservedly) broken by the floor.

Sitting up like the bad guy who simply won't lie down, my mother looked at me more out of pity than out of anger.

"God, ma," I said, stating the obvious, "I'm sorry, I must have slipped."

Slowly then we made it to our feet, careful not to bump against the pan.

I dusted her down, using the opportunity to check her for bruises, scratches, marks, maybe the telltale signs of ninja throwing-stars between her shoulder blades.

"I'm all right," she said, surprisingly unshaken. "But let that be a lesson to you now."

I exhaled for the first time in a minute. "I will," I said, "I will let it be a lesson."

And while I wondered what the lesson could have been, and what might be its practical applications, my mother said: "Now would you go and call the others down for tea."

At Your Convenience

When the first public toilet in the town had opened in February 1971, the headline in the local newspaper read, 'Momentous occasion in history of Portlaoise'. The following week's edition included a letter from a reader signed 'Yours in agony, Shortaken' pointing out that the 'loo' had inexplicably been locked on its maiden Saturday night, hardly the most convenient arrangement.

The debate over that first public toilet unbelievably had gone on for almost a decade, and not only in the local papers or County Council meetings (one hesitates to use the word Chamber in the context) but even in Dáil Éireann itself.

In June 1963, three months before I was born, Deputy Oliver J Flanagan questioned the Minister for Finance on the delay with an earlier version of the facility proposed for a location on the Abbeyleix Road. He received a long-winded reply from Minister O'Malley.

"In June, 1962, the Laois County Council applied for a site… The site, however, was not considered suitable… As a result of discussion with representatives… an alternative site… Subject to the concurrence… a formal offer… at an early date…"

Three years later the subject came up again for discussion in the Dáil, when references to "traffic considerations" proved to relate to passing cars and not the pedestrian traffic such a convenience might be expected to attract.

By coincidence my own interest in the subject goes back to almost precisely the same time. In 1966 I had been about three and was taken one day to the toilet by our neighbour Shirley Robinson, a girl a couple of years my senior and shortly thereafter to emigrate with her family to Australia. Though I can barely remember what she looked like, I clearly remember that particular visit because, just as we entered our big, strangely L-shaped bathroom (in which the toilet was enclosed in a confession box-like cubicle), Shirley looked me in the eye and asked me if I knew that it was haunted. The toilet was haunted. She herself had seen a ghost in there.

From that day on, even years later, long after the Robinsons had started over down under, I could not enter that bathroom or approach that toilet cubicle without feeling not fear but a kind of cold expectation, a physical hesitation however slight that would immediately make itself known—proof, if proof were needed, that words (good or bad, playful or serious) produce physical results.

Another reason why toilets have a particular interest for me has to do with my uncle Paddy and a story he brought home from his missionary work in the Kenyan bush. For there he found what he called an "ingenious" method to protect personal belongings from the attentions of others. One dug a small hole in the earth, placed the belongings inside, and then, well, um, proceeded to seal the vault. In part taboo, in part the threat of an unpleasant experience, the result was that objects secreted away in such a fashion would likely go undisturbed for years.

Unfortunately, this same general idea began to appeal to my father who, with a little tweaking here and there, saw that it might help to solve one of his own problems. For even he had come to realise by now that the embedding of broken glass along the perimeter wall of the old mill he used as a storeroom was less a deterrent to schoolboy intruders than an accident (and subsequent court case) waiting to happen. At no extra cost he could now see, the Borans of Kenya might teach the Borans of Ireland an important lesson in security.

But if this was the most extreme of my father's ideas—and among the most difficult to put into practice had the effort been made—it was not the most embarrassing of the incidents that relate to him and toilets. If the most common ingredient of toilet horror stories has to do with the blurring of the line between private and public, the incident with my father deserves special mention. That it also involves his teenage son makes it, to paraphrase the newspaper report quoted above, a momentous occasion in the history of myself.

For in June 1979, due to a postal strike, I got to accompany my father on a rare trip to Dublin—to collect, I believe, the tickets for some holidaymakers going out later that month. Having completed a number of other small drop-offs and collections, we arrived at the offices of Joe Walsh Tours on Baggot Street to be greeted by a sequence of impossibly glamorous receptionists,

"Hello, Nicholas, and you must be—?" my teenage awkwardness tying up my tongue.

But nothing one could not recover from in time, had my father not popped his briefcase up on the desk (my altar boy suitcase, as it had so recently been) and opening it to find his cheque book and good pen instead found himself blankly looking down, as did I—as did everyone else in the place—at the brand new toilet roll he'd brought with him from home, because, well, because you never know.

Taking the Train

Stories of the railway arriving into small Irish towns could in themselves supply a fascinating social history (much as the arrival of 'the electric' did a century later), but this must be left to a more diligent explorer than myself. For me, mention of the railway provokes a number of distinct and apparently unconnected images, as if in the undistinguished darkness of vague thought now and then I find myself pulling into a bright-lit station, hearing beyond the calming of the pistons the voices of strangers hardly known to me but somehow familiar.

Among that collection of images I would include the view from street level—and then from across the track itself—of that strikingly Gothic station house, and of the long-gone newspaper kiosk at the top of those limestone steps where sticks of Portlaoise rock and the Sacred Heart Messenger were to be found on sale, side by side, the latter suspended by black bulldog clips that looked to me (at six or seven years of age) like the mouths of the hounds of hell.

A favourite story, but from before my time, was of a station worker who was caught nibbling away on bottles of newly arrived whiskey and then replacing the missing inches of golden liquid with, well, his own recycled (once more distilled with feeling) version of same. How exactly he was rumbled my mother doesn't recall, but one imagines that the breaking news sent sales of whiskey plummeting in the town.

Then there was the youngster from a couple of miles out the Dublin side of town who, in my own time, as the train slowed into its approach, would jump off into the ditch to save himself the journey in and back out home again. Until one day… well, until one day the journey could no longer be completed in this world— the train thundering on ahead, the hedge, the ditch, the brambles and grass struck hard then falling still behind it, nature rushing in to fill the void…

In the mid 1970s onwards, when my father started to send me down to the station in the evening to collect some parcel or package (What's the difference?), there were sometimes as many as three or four dark-suited men hanging around waiting for the Mail Train in the barely heated office at the end of the platform, while Joe Campbell or one of the other guards took occasional phone calls that kept them abreast on the progress or lack of progress of the missing locomotive.

"She'll be another twenty minutes yet, young man," one of them might say, and nod towards a corner where I could sit and wait if I liked, though I seldom did. Hardly made any difference to sit it out inside, no one talking, or at least not that I could follow, the clock hands doing their noisy rounds, a sandwich on the counter turning up at the edges, an apple core gone black. Outside there were the lights of the town in the darkness of the countryside, our local Milky Way…

And there was the man with a snake in a wicker basket once, a man I sat in beside one day on the Limerick-Dublin train, on his way to see his mother, or so he said, which might have been a joke. Without the slightest warning suddenly he was showing me (and anyone who could bear to look) the sleeping coil of muscle just lying there. (A perfect Freudian moment that: one snake revealed while we were sat in the belly of another).

And I remember the ticket collector suddenly on his up the carriage—"Tickets, please. Have your tickets ready now, please"— and the Limerick lad's (illegal?) passenger, and the mouse which that passenger had just swallowed, quickly covered over again, stowaways in their world of dappled shadow…

And now the brakes of the thundering locomotive lock into place, squealing and throwing behind them along the tracks a fine mesh of sparks. The train stops, the doors wheeze open, and on the top of the Dead Wall, overlooking our whole lives, we step out of the belly of the beast to become in that instance ('Howaya, Paddy." "Howaya, Tom." "Just home for the weekend?" "Yeah?") ourselves again.

Exit

Not least because I grew up in a town famous for its prison, it seems ironic that on at least one occasion during my teenage years, I came close to being beaten up because of the word 'Exit'.

I'm not sure now which of us invented it, myself or one of the five or so close friends I hung around with at the time, but at one of those Sunday afternoon or early Friday evening discos in St. Mary's Hall, within yards of the prison, we found ourselves involved in, by any standards, an unusual pastime. Partly it was just for something to do, but mostly I think we wanted to defy the gang of 'hard men' who patrolled the edges of the dance floor in their Doc Martins, denims and leather jackets, like a gang of Neanderthal tax inspectors on a Sunday stroll.

The idea was simple: during a 'slow set', instead of asking a girl to dance (as few of us had the courage to do) or of loitering by the entrance to the ladies' toilets in the hopes of spotting the beautiful Lorraine Moran or some other lovely only ever briefly visiting our planet, without warning the small gang of us would leap up and out onto the dance floor, sending couples like startled cattle careering off to one side or other out of our way. And then we'd throw our arms wide in the air, or even more dramatically throw ourselves full-length down on the floor, a cross between a religious fundamentalist and a jubilant footballer, to offer our praises to, and hail (by times in a very loud voice) the object of our devotions.

"Exit, exit," we'd shout, pointing to the glowing sign over whatever door happened to be nearest, before one of the 'hard men' up dancing would signal to the others and we'd have to run for cover towards a clutch of supervising adults—bless you, Jimmy Keenan, Malcolm Smith.

The fact that we were shouting the word 'Exit' in a town famous for its maximum security political prison, and almost within earshot of that institution, may well have been the subconscious reason we were driven to it, as if we'd glimpsed and were now merely trying to point out to others the grim poetry of our dilemma.

As it was, most people—lovely Lips Lorraine among them—almost certainly dismissed us as fools. And most of the time we couldn't have cared less. We lived in a town whose only claim to fame was a prison, and of which *The Rough Guide to Ireland* a decade later would observe: "the main road by-passes it entirely and, unless you arrive by train and can't avoid it, you're probably well advised to do the same". If maintaining our sanity meant occasionally prostrating ourselves before electric signage at the local disco, or putting up with the verbal and physical assaults of local heavies who didn't even know what they were rebelling against, it was not only worth it but, in retrospect, was probably necessary.

St. Mary's Hall—or a version of it (strangely smaller)—lives on still, providing more or less similar release to a midland town's youngsters twenty-five years on. The music has changed, the seating, the lighting, the decor and, thank God, the toilets. And God alone knows what the fights are like there now, close up, when the threats are much darker than they ever appeared to us.

I was born a month to the day after St Mary's Hall first opened its doors, so I suppose more than most I sense there a version of the story of myself. Entering it now, it's hard not to hear the echo of thirty years ago, Chicago's horribly falsetto 'If You Leave Me Now', Queen's 'Bohemian Rhapsody' or Phil Lynott singing, half-threat, half-promise, "Tonight there's gonna be a jailbreak / somewhere in this town"—and none of us realising how right he was.

Just a few hundred yards away the steep, limestone walls of the prison itself, swept by searchlights, patrolled by shadows, scaled in dreams. But here in St Mary's, over each of the doors, like the ultimate in-joke or out-joke or no joke at all, that one word 'Exit', more commanding than ever, flickering still.

Vandals

Moustaches and goatee beards; pipes, glasses and missing front teeth; cowboy or occasionally pirate hats; arrows through the temples, bolts through the neck; these used to be and no doubt still are the standard textbook defacements practised in schools, the basic nouns in the young vandal's vocabulary.

Once I remember giving Savonarola a yellow afro hairdo, aided by the fact that the famous painting of him by Fra Bartolomeo showed him hooded, in profile, with plenty of the canvas left black. Most of the time, though, I can't claim any particular value for my interventions in the historical past, and there are sound arguments why history textbooks—why all textbooks for that matter—should be kept behind plate-glass like the Mona Lisa or on the top shelf like so many adult magazines.

One day someone—I have a face but no name—put the famous image of Jim Larkin, arms outstretched, on a crucifix, but perhaps this was not so much straightforward vandalism as a comment on the history of organised labour in a capitalist state.

At some point we'd all become aware of the stories of Christian Brothers and sexual impropriety, usually relating to other schools or to possibly mythical figures in the dark, historical recesses of our own. In second year I recall inventing a fictional cleric named Leotard Divestum, the hero of a number of short tales I would occasionally scribble on scraps of paper and pass around the class, the suggestive nature of his name being, I confess, the character's sole distinction.

Apart from such small-scale vandalism, I was never given to the defacement of school property, or any other property for that matter. The thrill of smashing half a dozen bottles lined up on a wall had been enough for me and had long since passed before I'd made it into double digits.

Though there was that one episode in the CBS Tower Hill which, from a distance at least, must have looked anything but accidental.

Heart of Glass

Was it my classmate Sean Bracken's steel-tipped brogue that did it, the slightest touch being enough to crack the glass and ignite a shower of transparent hail around us? Or could it have been something else entirely, the buckle of Brian Colbert's schoolbag or Dee Fennell's hurley coming into glancing contact with the pane? Or maybe it was a fault in the pane itself which at that precise moment as we gathered in front of it, fooling and jostling, passing the break-time minutes, at least one of us, ahem, idly swinging his foot...

Either way, what there was suddenly was an enormous crash, virtually an explosion, on that particular bright morning in 1979, that all of a sudden left the ground all around us, and even parts of our clothing, our hair and our faces covered in tiny cubes of shattered glass. The enormous floor-to-ceiling, ground-floor window of the school had been thoroughly smashed.

In addition to paying for it (which it was clear almost instantly we would have to do), our collective punishment—as advised with a slight smirk by Principal Boylan (known as The Long Lad or, simply, The Long) was that we ourselves should have the job of replacing it.

The principle (excuse the pun) of Offender Pays is a wise and just one, and one which even we could appreciate at the time. However, it did seem odd (then, and more so since) to entrust with its repair those who had just minutes earlier proved that their sole talent in relation to glass was for reducing it into a great number of pieces too small to serve any practical purpose. The sight of the almost impossibly tall brother speaking down to us then from his lofty perch unfortunately rendered this line of argument impossible to sustain.

And so it was that my friend and myself set off on foot to Centrepoint, the relatively new shopping complex which, despite its name, was still a fair walk out the Mountrath Road (carrying a load at least). Stopping brazenly, during school time, for ice-cream in Joe Dunne's, once arrived we ordered, watched it cut and then paid for the sheet of replacement glass in the hardware department, and without transport of any kind (and somehow never thinking to ask if we might have it delivered), with our hands wrapped in doubled-over cloths we set out on our Via Doloroso through Grattan Street, across the top square, and back down Main and Railway streets towards CBS Tower Hill, from a distance two teenage lads miming the transport of some giant object through the town, from closer up two red-faced, hunch-backed, sweating teens, lurching unsteadily under the considerable weight of an invisible burden, shuddering as the breeze changed direction or the uneven footpath outside Cooney's or Keegan's (Publicans and Undertakers) almost brought us to our knees.

The journey seemed to take most of the morning (which at least meant we were missing History and maybe even Maths). But somehow we made it there intact, and with the glass still intact. Steadily we placed it at a slight angle against the wooden frame of the window where we'd already chipped away all the old fragments with screwdrivers and a hammer, and now set about, gingerly, lifting into place the new 6ft by 5ft sheet which scraped and resisted here and there, but to our amazement (and despite our measurements) was fitting in, until one last tip of the hammer to tap just one last tiny tack flush into place was just too much for it. And for the second time in a day, we were once again standing out in a rainfall of glass, as if the skies had opened over us alone and showered us with imaginary raindrops, beautiful and square.

There are moments when the repeated failure of a mission becomes almost hilarious, and moments when it is close to terrifying. This was made up of both. Though we somehow managed to replace the replacement pane, to lock it in with enough putty to seal a mummy's tomb, we knew that some strange and unusual punishment must now await us.

And await us it did. A weekend in Carlow seminary, "where they make priests" someone joked, a joke at which none of us laughed.

When we got there, it wasn't as bad as we'd expected, but then again maybe we were still in shock. To our relief, we were given over into the care of a novice priest, originally from Portlaoise, who did his best to make us feel at home and, with late-night soft drinks in his room, almost independent, but the welcome didn't quite make up for the shock of early morning Matins or the horror that the Lord expected this kind of proof of commitment, day after day after day. If some of us had been growing bored at home, bored of the routine at school—bored even of the town itself—the experience quickly showed us it wasn't just any kind of change we were looking for.

That long weekend eventually behind us, soon we were happily back on planet earth again, somewhat singed by our close contact with Heaven, but relatively unharmed. And by the middle of that week it wasn't Gregorian chant—the *Jubilate Deo* none of us who had ears could quite resist—but the previous summer's *Let's All Chant* by the Michael Zaeger Band ("Your body, my body, everybody with your body...) that had us entranced. That, and the latest pop phenomenon from New York half-punk Blondie—every teenage boy's idea of salvation—filling the dance floor by the time we arrived in St. Mary's Hall (there's the welcome committee, Mick Larkin, Ray Kelly, Kevin McKeon and Vinny Whelan... all of them prancing around and lip-synching to beat the band): "Once I had a love and it was a gas, soon turned out had a heart of glass."

Goodbye, Mr. Chips

One lost the history papers he'd taken home for correction—in a freak windstorm on the golf course!

One was a close friend—as far as we were concerned, the certain lover—of another.

One would do two-fingered push-ups across the front row of desks and could connect almost any possible subject to his own personal favourites: ballistics and munitions.

One was the archetypal monster in the closet, a Golem-like figure who served his time in the claustrophobic bookshop underneath the stairs and about whom there was a near endless supply of whisperings and innuendo, any or all or none of which may have been true...

And one was so enthused by his subject he'd forget the whiteboard pens were water-soluble and, constantly damping his handkerchief with spittle, would end each lesson looking as if he'd been made up by a drunken beautician.

But in the St. Mary's CBS, the late Michael 'Chippy' O'Brien was, by any standards, an eccentric teacher, and not least for the fact that he encouraged the practice of giving nicknames, something rarely condoned by members of his chosen profession. Commander of some kind of Latinist force (as he seemed to regard himself), Chippy bestowed honours and derision in equal parts, and often simultaneously, on those he chose to so distinguish, numbering at least one Colonel, a Captain, a Keeper of the Door and a Baron among his retinue in our class.

Had we stopped to think that Maryborough in its time had seen numerous historical figures with such unlikely commissions and titles, we might not have been so surprised at Chippy's predilection for colourful nomenclature, his almost boyish delight in naming. Cursory research will quickly produce an impressive number of Colonels, Captains and Sheriffs by the score, and at least one Baron Maryborough in the pages of the history books. Of this last title (the one that amused us most, for some reason), the record states that it was granted in 1821 to the Right Honourable William Wellesley Pole, later the third Earl of Mornington, itself an appellation that might have suited the more sleepy-headed of Chippy's Latin conscripts, myself included. 'Ah, I see the Earl of Mornington has decided to grace us with his presence.' (That the same Earl/Baron was an elder brother of the Duke of Wellington might have suggested a number of other possible sobriquets, particularly in relation to those boys who hailed from the more rural outlying parts; for reasons best known to the Master, these went unexplored.)

In truth, Chippy's near obsession with names and naming seemed to derive from a wish to transport himself (and all of us) somewhere else entirely, miles from the shadow-laden, famine-era pile in which we found ourselves scrambling for sense to some semi-military outpost where ignorance was the enemy and control and authority the weapons by which it might be defeated.

By the time I came to St. Mary's the irony was that the meaning of Chippy's own nickname had long since been lost: only our parents—and only the brightest of them—knew what it meant. In fact it referred to the central character of a 1930s novel written by James Hilton in which a shy young teacher in a new job struggles to impose his authority on an unruly class. Had 'Chippy' ever been a shy young teacher thus confronted? Or was the nickname already tongue-in-cheek when first applied to him by a cast of press-ganged conscripts and raw recruits like ourselves who'd preceded us through those same panelled corridors to those same well-worn desks they'd inscribed with their names.

Chippy was authoritative, bordering on authoritarian in some matters—he liked to line up the weaker performers against the blackboard and, pacing back and forth in front of them, bark unanswerable questions like a Drill Sergeant in a Foreign Legion outpost. "Has Mr Boran, I mean to say, decided to develop his own dialect of Latin?" "Does the Captain have nothing better to do with his time than whisper sweet nothings into the Colonel's ear?"

In some of these encounters it was hard to remember that we were pupils in a modern school and not criminals awaiting trial and execution. Chippy himself sometimes seemed to be following a secret script, playing a kind of tormented Tommy Cooper character—the darkened side of his face made up for punishment, the bright, sometimes even winking side towards the rest of the room—ever the expert comedian, master of timing and stagecraft. In a word he appeared so much of the time to be acting, a player on a stage, that his familiar verbal tick—the recurrent, punctuating 'I mean to say…'—seemed less like something truly unconscious and more like some carefully chosen: for the star of the show the star's—I mean to say— catchphrase.

In many ways Chippy's behaviour verged on the surreal (in itself, one might argue, a kind of mind-control relying on shock tactics and the constant element of surprise). On one occasion, planning a school field-trip to "points south", including the Cliffs of Moher, he seemed seriously to consider the idea of bringing along a rope which he would thread through the sleeves of each member of the group lest any see fit to hurl himself into the ocean. Indeed, an ongoing worry about boys in his care plummeting to their deaths might help to explain his invariable request upon entering the classroom to his Keeper of the Door (and Windows) to close the latter in a timely fashion lest "any of the men be tempted to defenestrate".

Chippy was odd, hilarious by times, certainly a bit on the nutty side, sometimes embarrassing—but smart, ferociously smart. You knew that if the Romans ever finally invaded, here was someone who could be sent to deal with them. Not only could he speak their language, after all, but you got the distinct impression that he'd be happy at last to dress up in that fetching military clobber.

How his son Michael junior survived in a school where his father was such a headline attraction is a question for another time; but then how the children of even entirely unremarkable teachers (unremarkable people, for that matter) survive unscathed is a mystery to me.

Even so, the story of one's schooldays is, to a great extent, the story of one's encounters with that small group of adults who have a certain power afforded them and who wield it in their variously memorable ways. And it is hardly desirable, I mean to say it is hardly possible, to offer a sketch of that puzzling environment without including, what you might call, some form of portrait of the players on the stage.

And so, though I confess I was never particularly distinguished in any of Chippy's various subjects, it did occur to me bytimes that the conferring of the title Baron Boran might have reflected well on both of us, giving me some of the meaning I was after, and giving Chippy another word-gaming award.

But nothing came so easy in Chippy's class, in Chippy's service, in Chippy's world perhaps. Reward had to be earned, even if the rules were sometimes a good deal less than clear. Was the Captain, for example, *always* superior to the Baron? Did the Colonel continue to enjoy the support of his men despite injuring his arm in a bicycle accident (as Chippy would put it, "a diabolical assassination attempt")?

In the end perhaps that was his real legacy, for all his devotion to the military life: a chain of command that, when viewed from close up, proved somewhat illusory after all.

i.m. Michael 'Chippy' O'Brien, d. 22 November 2008

A Small-Town Hall

The gutters drip. The gutters drip and can be heard to drip so that after this week of endless rain the hall at the edge of town is like a ship after a storm has passed, a vessel thrashed and lashed and washed clean now and glowing, if not glowering, beneath a leaden sky.

And we're the teenage sailors, crew and steerage, transformed into adventurers by the turn of the key in Jo Hannon's hand, by the swing inward of the creaking door that turns the Macra na Feirme Hall into a craft that welcomes all aboard.

We are twenty or thereabouts in number, early to mid teens still, boys and girls, attention-seekers (like myself), wall-flowers and chaos-machines, front-line combatants all in the war between hormones and history, tradition and, well, new thrills. The soundtrack of our lives is highly sexualised, all bump and grind, more 'Hit Me With Your Rhythm Stick' than (given the venue) 'Do You Want Your Old Lobby Washed Down?'

But though we're teens and come across as loud and dull and rude and quick to take offence or retreat in petulance, we insist on being taken seriously: after all, we'll soon be twice the age that Dante was when he fell in love with Beatrice.

Even so, we're midland kids, small-town kids, and therefore (some say) safe enough from the troubles that in these dark days stalk the land: in other circumstances we might be old enough to play soldier and be brought to a hall like this at the edge of a town to train and ready ourselves to kill or to be killed...

Romance and war, love and death, Eros and Thanatos, the twin attractions every teenager feels more acutely because they're new to him, to her, the ghosts that stalk the streets of midland towns or lurk in the corners of a side-room of a country hall a microsecond after the switch is thrown, that is what we've come to investigate. That is why we call ourselves a club.

The endless patience and forbearance of the adults, Tom and Anne and Jo, the three of them sat on ice-cold stackable plastic chairs in a breath-visible room after dark, discussing choice, politics, sexuality and peace with a gang of spotty, awkward teens as if called back to the planet of their own adolescence to endure the torment of actually giving a damn.

Thought-games, mind-games, animations of various kinds and degrees of challenge. Jo with a scarf wrapped up to her ears in a big-buttoned herringbone coat with wide collars, Anne in a belted long tweed, Tom in a tweed jacket, leather-patched at the elbows, a mug of piss-weak tea held below his chin, probably for the heat alone...

And of what was said, and who said what, or who said what to whom, all of that is lost now, washed away now, like the storm waters absorbed into the earth that night, unbeknownst to us starting over their return journey to the sea... But from the sea to the sky, and from the sky, drip by tentative drip back to the land, before me here two decades later I watch again as the rain returns—as if only now completing its cyclic journey—and down this pane of glass before me runs a single raindrop, a single perfect tear, beyond which I can just about make out the shades and shapes of a gang of youngsters whose stillness in a darkened small-town hall belies the changes happening in their lives.

i.m. Jo Hannon, died December 16, 2008

Early Leavers

Lots of young lads I knew left or were taken out of school as soon as it was legal to do so. Usually this was just after their Inter Cert, which in any case was a basic requirement for many jobs and apprenticeships at the time. Had we been older and more comfortable with marking such transitions, on the last day of the exams we might have queued up to shake the hands of those early leavers, to wish them well, with a combination of envy and regret to send them on their way with one last joke, or shove or dead leg or manly hug disguised as a wrestling move.

As it was the moment came and went, and for the most part they drifted off up town or went back to stand out on the road and wait for their lifts back home as they always did, a nod from the rest of us as we passed as if it was just any other Friday afternoon.

One or two went to work on farms on in the family business, a small few more taking up apprenticeships with one of the few 'solid employers' around the town. Some went to Dublin, one or two as far as England as their fathers and uncles had done a generation before. And a small few others just hung around the town with lads a couple of years older than themselves, wondering what exactly they were supposed to do now with the wide world spread before them.

It was always strange to meet these lads whom one knew so well and now suddenly did not know, as though between us a solid if transparent screen had been quietly erected. Off on some after-school joinery delivery, my father might pull in for petrol somewhere around the town and I would find to my surprise holding the pump not some old oil-skinned friend of his but a young, oil-skinned friend of mine, a man now where I was still a boy.

The opening minutes were nearly always awkward: How was so-and-so, a mutual friend? Any news of Mr X, a favourite or most despised teacher? And they were awkward not least because already we could sense how little we had in common, how the world of school and the world of work (despite our time together) were light years apart even in a town as small as ours.

"She's a bit low in the back there," he'd say, catching me by surprise; or "You might be looking at a new fan belt for her, Mr B"—as if he was talking about a woman and not a car and addressing, as I suddenly realised, my father now and not his schoolboy son.

And when *his* father would come out of the back room, wiping his oily hands on a roll of paper, my friend would do his best to hold his own, looking off into the distance and delivering the line that, for once and for all, confirmed he was now one of them: "Could be fine," he say, "later on, if it doesn't rain."

And as we'd be making to leave, to get back on the road—tyres at their optimum, new fan belt in place, the windscreen wiped clean with a dripping sponge—instead of shaking my hand he'd just nod and stand to one side, and then in the rear-review mirror, overalls bunched around his ankles, he'd give me a grin followed by his old man's salute.

Bogmen

Forty shades of grey or grey-brown. And an ice-blue sky above it. That's what the bog was. And when we went out there to work as summertime bogmen, we might as well have been walking out onto the surface of the moon. When a sudden torrential downpour meant you couldn't see your hand or foot in front of you, like teenage conscripts at the Somme you ran blindly ahead, hoping for sanctuary in a small galvanized shed, but expecting at any moment the ground to open up and swallow you whole.

But first thing in the morning, the enormous visual sweep of it all. Nothing taller than the low walls we had the day before laboured to build. The entire landscape flat like the bed of a lake— which was exactly what it was, or had been, once upon a time. The county most cut off from the sea, with a dried-up seabed at its heart: surely one for the books.

A meadow pipit sang somewhere, *tsi, tsi, tsi,* relentlessly; dragonflies bigger than anything you might see in town already up and hovering in front of your face; a hare darting past your peripheral vision as you left the beauty of ling heather, bog cotton, bog rosemary or asphodel behind to enter the churned-up, cut-back, stripped-bare heart of the county—the sodden peat itself.

Sodden in the sense of being wet through and through, and almost impossible heavy; sodden too because it had been cut into sods, long before we'd ever been engaged, poor sods that we were, to take it on. And thus we began to assume our positions in the post-dawn light, like so many ancient Egyptian slaves, expected to erect great monuments in that most hostile of places.

Some lads were cut out for work on the bog, some weren't. Fellows like Eamon 'Togher' Dunne had been named for the place, a togher being an ancient road through the bog. Townies like us were never going to compete.

One of Robert Frost's most famous poems, 'Mending Wall', starts with the line: "Something there is that doesn't love a wall". It might have been written for myself and Gerard 'Herbie' Ennis, my pop music-obsessed sidekick who, like me, had avoided bogs in his formative years and was determined to make this summer of futile labour result in a sun tan, at the very least.

So while others typically arrived long before us, and would be up to their knees in belching bog holes trying to retrieve the remains of their collapsed pillars of Hercules, the moment we breezed in Herbie and myself would shrug off our backpacks, unscrew our flasks and delight in the magic of a fresh brew of tea in the great outdoors. And through the wonders of technology, in what looked like an apocalyptic wasteland, the 2FM DJ would helpfully segue between 'Reunited' by Peaches and Herb (Herbie's current favourite, naturally) and 'Death Disco' by PIL, the sound of the latter in the unreal air enough to bring shouts of approval from Eamon Duff across the trenches that separated our ruined island of lotus-eating with the surrounding Manhattan skylines of turf.

"Well, dogs," someone would say, "how ye gettin' ahn today?" imitating some lifelong bogman all the country lads recognised, one of the many hunched, slow-moving figures that would turn up in the one hut for miles during a thunderstorm, filthy as a miner, soft-spoken as a priest, and interested only in local hurling politics and the specific attributes of the latest resident of Page 3.

"What would you make of her now?" someone would ask, pointing to the latest pair of naked bosoms to grace the altar of the hut. Outside lightning danced off the peat, attracted, or so it was said, by something in its mineral composition. "Begor, men," the old-timer would respond, clearing his throat of dust. "She'd haveta watch herself if she kem out here done up like that."

"Hard to believe he's only forty-five, fifty at the most," someone would remark, as the 'old-timer' headed away back to his plot. And we'd be left there wondering how the same bog that could preserve oak and butter and all sorts of stuff might leave a middle-aged man like that looking as old as Methuselah.

Sometimes I wondered if these old lads had, like us young bucks, started out on the bog as a way to pass the time, to pass a summer or two lifting the water-heavy machine-cut turf into low walls, then coming back to it later in the season when the top had gone grey and dry and crisp, when a lightness had crept into it, to expose its hidden underside to the air. In truth, few of them had the choices we had: working on the bog was more likely a role they'd inherited, a tradition that had been in their families for the hundreds of years men had been out cutting and 'footing' turf.

I wondered what they did when the season ended, these so-called old timers, after the youngsters had scrubbed themselves clean and gone back to school, when the small transistor radios chirping out 'Reunited' or 'Death Disco' in the shimmering distance had been replaced with, well, nothing but primordial silence, a silence broken only by the tattoo of rain on a galvanized roof and then, away in the distance, the summer come round again, the radio once more bringing with it the welcome voices of youth, and the beat of Michael Jackson's latest incarnation.

i.m. Michael Merriman

Escape from Secondary School

When the Careers Guidance teacher visited our class and asked us what we wanted to be, Noel Rowe wrote down "brain surgeon". We laughed for a week. The only time most of us took school seriously was when we seriously wanted to escape.

Sometimes I imagined making a bomb. Maybe we all did. In the chemistry lab, Tom Bleach's class, we listened carefully in case 'The Bah' as we called him might inadvertently disclose the ingredients for a home-made device with which we could blow the back wall clear off the building, then shimmy down a drainpipe into Tower Hill, clouds of debris and chalk dust in our wake.

I wanted to pull up the loose floorboards in Room 5A and drop down into the empty classroom below while the poor wretches were out playing Gaelic games in their gooseflesh uniforms in the swamp that passed for a field.

At the very least I wanted to organise a strike, a sit-in, a day of silence or its opposite, a day of roaring, screeching electric guitars with my friend Paschal Sheeran on the bass doing his best axe-murderer stare. And failing that we could at least organise a walk-out, the erection of barricades, a march through the town to match the Republican marches.

Unfortunately for me, at 15 or 16 or 17 the only thing I had the slightest interest in was music—a subject not available in the school—and the day I looked forward to was the day I'd leave my tattered and half-read textbooks behind for the next generation of manacled schoolboys in whose bedrooms too starburst electric guitars would lie on unmade beds all day like lovers waiting for their loved ones to come home.

Roundabout

On summer evenings we sit on the back of a concrete bench in front of the Marian Shrine in the Market Square, watching cars go by and—from the time of its appearance in 1977—circling the town's first roundabout before driving away.

How difficult it would be to say exactly what we talk about here that makes us any different from other similar groups of youngsters in any other midland or coastal town, in Ireland or anywhere else on the inhabited earth. Girls, music, the moon and stars overhead…? Makes of cars and motorcycles; scores in some hurling or football match, our school against some other school, Clonad against the town; town characters like the Arab Shea, the Kettle Flynn or Mena Fortune, the ancient, lace-skinned newsagent with the movie-star name…

We talk about the Courtney Bros Circus and the elephant they've just paraded up the back road of the town. We talk about movies, Bruce Lee, new brands of chocolate bar, the IRA, Moscow, the Vietnamese 'boat people' selling noodles in their small van in the Square. We talk about Tony Shelley, our elderly neighbour on Main Street, who died at the beginning of the summer and was buried, everybody says, in the coffin he'd kept underneath his bed for years.

And we talk about girls, girls in general, and yes specific girls.

We use each other's names sometimes, nicknames other times, have weeks where we call each other 'Dog' and nothing else, punctuating our exchanges with laughter, roars, groans and shouts, all the aural decoration of a band of thriving young lads on a balmy evening with little that is urgent on their minds.

Looking back at it, more than the detail what I see is what we've learned to call (following our American cousins) the big picture.

For at the heart of even small-town life is an enormous mystery every generation must find a name for. For us, for that time at least, it was called The Roundabout. And at a certain time of day, of life, there is nothing one can do but submit to its spell, its hypnotic lure or strange attraction. "Ma, I'll see you later, I'm going up town." And nothing one could wish for but the company of friends (bright lights every one) to trick and distract, to tease and taunt, and at last to just sit with and stare into the dark and turning heart of what we are.

The Swarm

At some point some of the town's hard men rebranded themselves as The Swarm, after the horror film of the same name in which a swarm of killer bees inexplicably—and quite unprovoked—attacks a sleepy Texan town with predictably disastrous results.

My classmate Con H_____ was widely reputed to be a member (if formal membership there was) and, despite not being the oldest, was even said by some to be its leader. And, yes, he was no pushover and had grown-up, street-wise brothers on his side, but the fact that he was my classmate—and on occasion my sparring partner in our weekly karate class—meant I found it hard to be worried about not getting home while others of my acquaintance, on occasion, would opt for the scenic route.

The Swarm, it seems, were particularly unimpressed by kids who were not particularly impressed by The Swarm—which is how it goes when you're the only show in town. And like all gangs that don't strictly police their numbers, The Swarm included in its ranks both good-natured youngsters, opting out for a while, as well as a handful of others looking to proclaim their courage from the safety of a crowd.

Comprised as it was of such a wide cross-section of the town's young manhood, one might argue that The Swarm didn't exist at all, at least until other youngsters—and then the wider population—began to use the name. This is one of the reasons, I suppose, why I resisted it, even as a useful shorthand to describe a vaguely threatening gathering up ahead. For without a cool-headed review of each situation as it presented itself, every young lad loitering in a doorway on a miserable night became a lookout or crouched assassin, the end result being that we'd have to ring the entire town with walls and bars, in the style perhaps of our already famous prison.

Frankly, I found it impossible to imagine that bright-eyed Con—Con of the flowing mane and manly build (a cross between Geronimo and Johnny Cash)—could ever have had time for many of the guys to be observed trailing him around, less like killer bees than chicks or ducklings. I found it hard to understand why lads I liked, and liked a lot, when on their own seemed to shut up shop and hang the Closed sign in the window when they hung out with the other so-called members of the gang. If gangs were about anything they ought to offer ampification rather than dilution.

And that was when it struck me, just how many connections were there really between the fictional, Hollywood *Swarm* and this Irish midlands tribute act that so many people wished would just buzz off.

For a start, there was the matter of the two towns at the heart of the stories. In the movie version, after attacking a military base in Texas, the swarm of (South American, as it happens) killer bees quickly moves on to lay siege to the nearby small town of Marysville. In our case, the small town suffering the infestation was (formerly known as) Maryborough.

Then there was the matter of the military base where the movie begins, a base which, for all intents and purposes, could have been Portlaoise Prison, right down to the fact that (as in one famous escape attempt about this time) its main gate is inexplicably left ajar. ('All Weapons, Explosives or Incendiary Devices May Be Confiscated' reads a sign on the facility's front wall. Given the level of smuggling in Portlaoise in the late 1970s, a similar sign might not have done any harm.)

Killer bees, bewildered extras, puzzled boffins... And, in Portlaoise, young lads in doorways smoking and telling jokes to pass the time.

At this point one might fairly ask if the scene in which the movie swarm is seen to attack a school full of ten-year-olds might really have provided the inspiration for the naming of the gang? Are not all such gangs, at one level or another, the continuation of an unchecked childhood desire to do harm to the world? Certainly there was at least one individual hanging around with The Swarm who, even as a very young lad, still in short pants, had been kicking out at others, hurting others indiscriminately and, as he'd done when he'd beaten me up manym, many years before, whistling like an altarboy as he walked away. If people ever feared The Swarm, it was kids like him they feared, and would have been wise to fear either in a gang or on his own: the name was little more than a name.

And yet the name was also an identity. And kids with nothing better to do, no less than kids with plenty on their cards, were entitled to one as well.

If, in due course, the Marysville (Texas) Flower Festival inevitably attracts the fictional swarm (black dots painted directly onto celluloid, and the illusion is complete), what conditions provided the lure to our own apian scourge? With no such festival taking place back then around the town, among the few opportunities for a volatile crowd to gather was at the Stradbally Steam Rally dances out the road.

And in fact it's true that there in the windswept, beer-slippery marquee, and on more than one occasion, members of the gang did indeed end up trading blows with members of the public, and even with themseles, while undaunted behind them Country & Irish stalwarts in their rhinestone-encrusted blouses and wide-brimmed hats continued to pedal their waltz-time wares, only marginally more up tempo than before.

From the Flower Festival the fictional swarm move on to bigger things. Following the initial attacks which have Texans running in all directions shouting "Get inside, get inside", the confusion escalates into outright chaos. With the swarm, well, swarming—and for reasons best known to the director—next up are scenes in which brave army lads sporting smart new flame-throwers illogically burn Houston to the ground.

"Its size is immesurable, its power is limitless, its enemy is man," the voice-over enthuses. Michael Caine, Richard Widmark, Katharine Ross and Henry Fonda are among the normally capable actors whose variety of concerned expressions suggest they are trying their best to make sense of the plot.

The movie of *The Swarm* has more holes in it than a honeycomb. Corpses from one scene are on their feet in the next. In one major conflagration scene a camera crew is visible in a shop window, fire extinguishers in hand. It's hard to know, or care, if they're trying to help to put out the fire or burn the studio to the ground.

As it transpired, the Portlaoise Swarm gradually faded away. One minute we were all talking about them, one minute about something else. All of a sudden the name seemed unlikely, bizarre, even foolish. Younger kids were heard to make jokes—"'S'warm tonight, isn't it?" "Tis, 's'warm all right"—after which, well, the game was up.

To stop their march (so to speak) in the movie version, Henry Fonda and his colleagues resort to milking the bees of their venom, hoping to devise an antidote. In Portlaoise, for various reasons, this was not tried.

"The African killer bee portrayed in this film bears absolutely no relationship to the industrious, hard-working American honey bee to which we are indebted for pollinating vital crops that feed our nation." So reads the disclaimer at the end of *The Swarm*. I sometimes wonder if any of the members of the Portlaoise gang ever stayed all the way to the end, long enough to see that message roll. If they had done, they might have taken it, and themselves, less seriously.

My Father and Jules Verne

My father and Jules Verne were linked in some strange way. For a start, though I didn't discover the fact until recently, my father was born on March 24, the anniversary of Verne's death, and died on February 8, the anniversary of Verne's birth.

Jules Verne put people in capsules and sent them twenty thousand leagues under the sea. He dangled them from balloons or, by various means, had them circumnavigate the globe in 80 days. My father, being a small-town travel agent, also sent people on journeys, though seldom farther than to Lourdes on the annual parish pilgrimage.

Madam Verne once said of her famous partner: 'My husband has never re-read a chapter of a single one of his stories. When the last proofs are corrected, his interest in them ceases.' My father too kept voluminous files and papers in his office in the house where I grew up. Equally, he was not inclined to revisit them, except where absolutely necessary. But unlike Verne, my father's memory was not always what it might have been.

Even in his healthier years, my father was inclined to misplace things: his glasses, his many keys, his favourite brown-handled knife. Early on he joked that someone (usually my mother) was hiding them from him; with the passing years he seemed to believe this more and more.

But the first sure sign that my father's memory was beginning to fail came on his return from a holiday abroad, and, dates and other coincidences aside, might have separated himself and Jules Verne forever.

My sister Margaret had been teaching English in Portugal and invited my parents to join her for a short holiday. To everyone's surprise, my father turned his back on the unfinished paperwork, and away they went.

As in Lourdes each year, in Portugal my father rediscovered the attractions of wine, and reportedly spent a fair amount of the time there happily gliding across the surface of the days. The brown-handled knife might have been produced to skin one of the attractive-looking oranges in their host's apartment—which embarrassingly proved to be a balsa wood ornament that forever afterwards would bear the scars—but this was by far the worst catastrophe to befall him. At least until their return to Dublin.

At the airport, the two happy travellers were met by my other sister Mary and her husband Pat. In good form, and in good time, they were driven to Hueston station to catch the Portlaoise train. But it was at the station that my father's memory gave up on him. Where was his travel pass?

My father suggested my mother had it. My mother insisted my father had. My father checked his coat pockets, two outside, two inside, all of them full of various notes and scraps. But no sign of the pass. With the train rapidly filling within sight, my sister suggested my father remove his overcoat and, systematically, try his jacket pockets. My father searched each pocket in turn—old envelopes, various keys, the brown-handled knife—but still no pass. Then it was down to his waistcoat and pants pockets, still with no luck.

By now both he and my mother were showing signs of travel fatigue. My father was certain someone had taken the pass. My mother knew otherwise. My sister intervened. With the train rapidly filling alongside them, she approached a station official, explained that her parents had just returned from a holiday abroad and my father couldn't find his pass. No problem, said the ticket checker, generously ushering them towards the train. They could find it in transit and everything would be OK.

At last my parents boarded the train, my mother looking tired and exasperated, my father, no doubt, suitably embarrassed, still insisting he'd done nothing wrong.

My sister and her husband stood on the platform, relieved to have the two travellers installed on the last leg of their journey. They watched my parents find a seat by the window and, with just seconds to go before the train's departure, deliver themselves into it.

Jules Verne was born in Nantes. My mother's name is Nancy; my father called her Nance. Other similarities may well exist that I have yet to discover, though, in all likelihood, none of them will amount to much.

But re-reading Verne's best known adventure recently, I noted with amusement a train departure scene early on in the book. Just before Phileas Fogg and his servant Passepartout embark on their great round-the-world trip, Passepartout utters a sudden cry of despair.

"Alas! In my hurry—I—forgot—"

"What?" asks Mr Fogg.

"To turn off the gas in my room," replies the servant.

"Very well, young man," returned Mr Fogg, coolly; "it will burn—at your expense."

In the case of my father, it was not so much a memory of something forgotten that suddenly returned as the forgotten thing itself.

As my sister and her husband stood watching, a whistle was blown somewhere, the train shunted once or twice and at last began to move. My mother looked out of the window at my sister and her husband and gave a little royal wave. It was only then that my father, still looking sheepish, reached up to remove his hat, and, from the top of his head, like a solitary flake of confetti, the missing travel pass drifted back slowly to earth.

Number 74

Just a few days before our old house was due for demolition, I announced my intention to go back there with a screwdriver. For reasons I couldn't explain at the time, the idea of unscrewing the old brass numbers 7 and 4 from the hall door and taking them away with me before the bulldozers might move in, was proving irresistible.

What gave the idea a sense of necessity was that, earlier that same morning, lying in bed in the late morning in my mother's still unfamiliar new house about a quarter of a mile away, I'd been struck out of the blue by the memory of a poem we'd learned in secondary school, almost 20 years before, Shakespeare's 'Sonnet LXIV':

> When I have seen by Time's fell hand defaced
> The rich proud cost of outworn buried age;
> When sometime lofty towers I see down-razed
> And brass eternal slave to mortal rage...

Apart from the sharp hard music of those lines which have never left me, there was the double meaning in that word 'razed' which sounded like but was, apparently, the exact opposite of its homophone, 'raised'. That something could be flattened while sounding like it was being lifted up was a cruelty inherent in language that could hardly be ignored. If the bulldozers were going to 'raze' our old house to the ground, then I had no real choice but to go and 'raise' the number 74 to a whole new level.

For all the obvious reasons, and over more than three and a half decades, the number 74 had come to mean a lot to me. In the long litany that used to include Ireland, Europe, the Earth, the Solar System, the Milky Way, immediately after my name —always the point of departure—the number 74 was the most important single other fact. Mystical before I knew the meaning of that word, the number was something without which I was not properly connected to the universe and would forever be condemned to drift like some Dickensian ghost in and out of all the rooms of the world, looking for my final resting place. The actual house that was 74 Main Street might long have been a big, cold, run-down jumble of winding stairs and draughty rooms, shortly to be a demolition site behind lace curtains, but the thing that was conjured by the mere mention of the number was something not so easily erased.

When I first informed my mother of my plan, she laughed then tried to change the subject. Was she genuinely afraid, as she claimed, that someone might confront me in the act of removing those two-inch brass numbers? The new owner or one of his representatives? Was it possible she could really have feared that even such minor tampering might bring about the collapse of the deal that had, almost magically, at last given her a new house, a new home, in exchange for an old one that might otherwise have become her tomb? Though she had more than risen to the challenge of starting over after her husband's ongoing illness, there must have many terrifying moments when she wondered if she could really cope on her own again.

And if the number 74 represented some three and a half decades for me, for her it represented almost double that length, its removal marking the end of not just one but of many eras, and of many buildings in a sense: her girlhood home, her maiden house, the castle of her marriage and motherhood, the haunted edifice that might have been her later years there alone.

It took me, I think, a whole evening to persuade her that taking those two numbers back would be an act of reclamation, of psychic repossession, as well as an act of acceptance.

Thus, as they say of such momentous occasions, it came to pass. Resistance was removed, permission granted. Without making too much of it, I put on my coat, zipped up high to cover the bulge of the large, red-handled screwdriver I carried in my inside pocket, and I set out on the short journey up the town, part hit-man, part thief.

The deed itself took just a couple of minutes, though I seemed to be there an age, standing on the footpath before that door that had once led into a life which seemed now, bizarrely, like a fiction. It was just after seven in the evening, and still bright. A dog stopped to look at me, but of the people passing no one paid any attention. I felt, for a moment, as if I were invisible, as if anyone who did bother to stop and look would have seen only four tiny screws slowly unscrewing themselves from the hardwood door, to be followed by the number 7 and the number 4, all of them together in a little floating cluster, a little brass solar system, one by one disappearing into the black hole of my inside pocket to be spirited away to a future unimaginable from there.

7 and 4: special, even sacred numbers. And when I go home these days and look at them now, screwed into place on the door of my mother's new kitchen, in my mother's new house, and I see her smiling across at me, years later already but still enjoying the joke, it's as if, thanks to love, we might at any moment step back, if not quite into our old lives, then at least through one of the many doorways of the heart.

Bloody Waste of Time

After a long illness, in 1999 my father finally passed away. And as anyone who's suffered the loss of a family member knows, you feel it in unexpected, unpredictable ways.

Despite his small-farm background, my father had somehow ended up marrying a townie and settling into married life in our big old three-storey house on Main Street, maybe only twenty miles but a world away from his place of origin. For that reason, perhaps, there were quite a few townie things he failed to develop a feel for. Among them one might include the backing of horses.

Given that our family lived right in the middle of Main Street, it wasn't all that strange that our front windows looked directly out at the premises of the bookmaker Paddy Power. Yet despite its proximity, and despite the fact that so many of my father's friends could be seen to frequent it, to the best of my knowledge my father never went in there except to bring us over in turn to place a few pence on the Grand National when we were kids.

Gambling for my father was, like pop music and going to the pictures (and no few other things) 'a bloody waste a time.'

And so how strange that, just one month after his death, our house—which had been sold and demolished during his two-and-a-half year illness—should have been replaced by a brand-new building, the first tenant of which was the bookmaker Paddy Power.

Within weeks of its opening, down visiting my mother in her new house for the day, I made a point of going up to survey the changes and to place my own small bet as if, in some way, the story of that house and my father's time inside of it might be completed.

After standing opposite for a few minutes to review the new concrete facade, the raised ceilings where three storeys had become two, and strangest of all by far the new signboard, I steeled myself, crossed the street and entered.

Inside, the decor was unrecognisable—television screens lined up along one wall; newspaper betting pages tacked on to a noticeboard that ran the length of the other; three girls behind a high counter, all of them wearing spotless white shirts and intent on their business. And, of course, a number of faces I recognised from years of looking out of our front window were there. And a good number of others nowhere to be seen.

And then I looked up. And my heart almost stopped.

"I bet I know what you'll be puttin' your few bob on," said a man I half recognised. But I was unable to answer him. For I had just then seen that, running in the 2.00 o'clock at Newbury—first horse on the card in fact, its name currently blazing from every second television screen in the room—was a horse by the name of *Borani. Borani, the Borans!* This was it, surely, an unmistakable sign!

I staggered to the counter, ransacking my pockets as I went. It was two minutes to two. I'd only a ten-pound note and a handful of odd coins. If I'd had a thousand pounds I would have put it on that horse. The name Boran is unusual, to say the least; *Borani* I have never come across. And that this horse should be running right now, in this one race I'd decided in advance to bet on, and here on the site of the very place where my father had brought the name from country to town, from single man to married couple to extended family, from singular to plural... *Borani...* My God, my whole family, my very DNA, was involved in this!

My heart was pounding. My mouth was dry. My legs were, literally, shaking.

"And... they're off."

Almost as soon as I heard the words it was if I'd been slapped in the face, snapped out of a dream. Though I tried to hold back the knowledge, tried to keep it to some part of my mind where I wouldn't have to deal with it, I knew what was about to happen.

And long before they entered the final furlong it was clear to me that not only would Borani not *win* the 2.00 o'clock at Newbury but he wouldn't even be placed—("And it's Grinkov followed by High and Mighty in second place, followed by King Darius in third and…)

And as horse after horse after horse crossed over the line, it started to look possible he might not even finish.

"Good money," my father chose his moment to whisper in my ear, evidently enjoying himself wherever he was now. And we both said it together as I tore up my betting slip: "Gambling? Bloody waste of time."

Envoi

Chucky-Chucky-Four-Corners. It was the name of a game that preoccupied us for days and months and years in primary school, even during school holidays, a game where one person stood in the middle of a square, with four others standing at the corners, and the one in the middle had to intercept two of the others who, on an agreed signal, would make a dash to swap places.

Birds singing in the fields beyond St Brigid's Place, beyond the prison, and every young lad in the school yard or out on the road shouting Chucky-Chucky, Chucky-Chucky till their throats hurt.

Then, as now, the meaning of it was beyond me. It can hardly have been related to the other word *chucky*, a term for a country hick or bumpkin which I'm sure in any case was an invention of my sister's and didn't come into being until some years after the time I'm thinking of.

And, I suppose, it would be too much altogether to imagine that it might have something to do with the Irish word *tiocfaidh*, as in the Republican motto *Tiocfaidh ár Lá, Our day will come*. Childhood play is hardly immune from historical or political influence (think of 'Ring a Ring o' Roses' and all those ghoulish Victorian nursery rhymes), but even in the absence of other theories it would be hard to sustain such an interpretation on the basis of guesswork alone.

In the end, I suppose, these odd fragments of childhood experience have to work out their own meanings. Certainly I cannot now think of Chucky-Chucky-Four-Corners without imagining that, unbeknownst to us all, the boys standing on the four corners, calling to each other, were for all the world like so many prison officers or army soldiers manning their lone observation posts.

And the boy in the middle, pacing back and forth and side to side, looking for just a glimmer of a chance, I see that kid as, well, the prisoner inside the prison, but also maybe as a version of myself, not trapped in the invisible prison of the past any more so much as visiting again briefly for one more look, still trying to puzzle it out, to make some sense of it all this time, and free-associating there for all he's worth:

tiocfaidh ár lá, chucky-chucky-four-corners,
chucky four green fields, chucky the green fool;
chucky fool's gold, chucky gold stars,
chucky star light, chucky light years...

Walking Up Main Street

One time you couldn't walk up Main Street—because you couldn't walk, you hadn't learned to walk, you were a baby in your mother's pram or father's arms. It was all done for you, all done to you, it was all about you.

Another time you couldn't walk up Main Street—because you had to stay where you were put, inside the house, looking out the window, out of harm's way, the front door kept securely shut.

Another time you couldn't walk up Main Street without some other youngster coming over to you and saying, "Ya Lookin'? Did you say something about my mother?"

Another time you couldn't walk up Main Street because you couldn't be bothered.

Another time it rained so much you spent three whole days without so much as stepping out onto Main Street.

Another time you couldn't walk up Main Street because you were living in a tower block in another country, twelve hours away by bus and train and tube and foot and creaking, always sticking lift.

Another time you couldn't walk up Main Street because you were back in a flat in Dublin, and you were busy, licking your wounds, playing the blues, reading the poems from the prison that was Eastern Europe, finding something that you needed hidden in the open there.

Another time you couldn't walk up Main Street without someone saying 'Howya, Paddy' or 'Howya, Pat, haven't seen you around in years', and you only visiting for a few hours and wishing you didn't have to choose between time with old friends and time with your family, and time just standing doing nothing at all on Main Street.

Another time you couldn't walk up Main Street because, as soon as you stepped off the bus and came down Lyster Lane, one of those old friends appeared, opened the door of his car and whisked you away to your mother's *new* place, bypassing Main Street entirely so that you drove through a town you scarcely recognized.

Another time you couldn't walk up Main Street because you were walking down Main Street, slowly, behind a hearse, seeing the ghosts at all the windows, hearing a voice that used to be yours decades earlier quietly whispering the names: Miss Cussen, Peggy Meehan, Sally and Sean Dempsey, Mick and Biddy Lynch, Eilie Whelan, Mena Fortune, Sheila and Paddy Clear…

Another time, down for a day, you were on your way towards Main Street, certain that something would interrupt you, someone would call your name, the clouds would break… But nothing happened. As if you weren't there, as if you didn't exist at all, the street absorbed you, forgave you then went on about its business. And you, you walked up Main Street, were carried along through Main Street, drifted up the notion of a Main Street—its gently-curving lines and light-filled windows—in your lonely procession of one.

NOTES

PAGE NO.

54   *Logue's Homer: War Music.* Faber & Faber, 2001.

90   Diarmuid Coffey. *O'Neill & Ormond: A Chapter in Irish History,* Maunsel & Company Ltd., 1914

164   *The Dimension of the Present Moment* is the title of a collection of essays by the late Czech poet and immunologist, Miroslav Holub.

Dedalus Press
New Writing from Ireland and the world

Established in 1985, the Dedalus Press is one of Ireland's best-known literary imprints, with a particular interest in contemporary Irish poetry and poetry from around the world in English translation.

For further information on Dedalus Press titles, or to visit our Audio Room of free-to-download recordings by many of the writers on our list, see **www.dedaluspress.com**